An Introduction to

PERSIAN LITERATURE

PUBLISHER'S NOTE

The manuscript of this book was delivered to the publisher shortly after the death of the author in September, 1966. In preparing the manuscript for the printer, UNESCO and the publisher have had the generous help of Ehsan Yar-Shater, Hagop Kevorkian Professor of Iranian Studies in Columbia University, whose contribution to the final form of the text is gratefully acknowledged.

An Introduction to
PERSIAN
LITERATURE

by Reuben Levy

COLUMBIA UNIVERSITY PRESS
New York and London   1969

Reuben Levy (1891–1966) was Professor of
Persian in the University of Cambridge

Copyright © 1969 UNESCO
Library of Congress Catalog Card Number:
68–8876
Printed in the United States of America

CONTENTS

CONTENTS

An Introduction to

PERSIAN LITERATURE

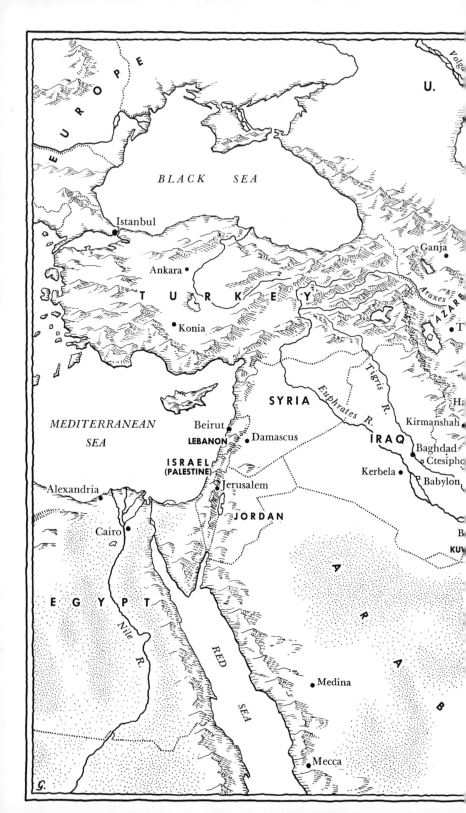

S. S. R.

ARAL
SEA

Khwarazm

Samarqand

TRANSOXIANA

CASPIAN SEA

TURKMENISTAN

Oxus R.

Jaxartes R.

Merv

Balkh

Gurgan

Tus
Mashad

Nishapur

Kabul

Qazvin

TABARISTAN
(MAZANDERAN)

Herat

AFGHANISTAN

Ghazni

Tehran

KHURASAN

IRAN

Isfahan

(PERSIA)

P A K I S T A N

Indus River

Persepolis

Shiraz

FARS

PERSIAN
GULF

Karachi

Muscat

ARABIAN

SEA

A

········· Present-day boundaries

0   500 Miles

ONE: THE HISTORICAL
SETTING

Persia, known to its own citizens as Iran, is a country which lives, like its one-time rival Greece, with the light of a brilliant past upon it. Today its ancient boundaries have receded. The writ of its emperor, the "shahanshah" (king of kings), no longer runs as once it did "across the River (Oxus)" or into the "Land of the Two Rivers (Tigris and Euphrates)." Tradition and legend preserved in Persian literature assert that in ancient days the river Oxus marked the untransgressable dividing line between Iran and Turan, that is, between the land of the Persians and that of their hereditary foemen, the Turcomans.

In the period 224–651, when the shahs of the Sasanian dynasty held sway in Iran and disputed with Byzantium

For the sake of readability diacritical marks on transliterated Persian names and words have not been used in the main body of this work. However, the Persian letter *'ayn* (') and the hiatus between two long vowels, the *hamza* ('), have been retained.

I

for the mastership of the Middle East, they numbered within their realm a string of provinces which are today included within the Soviet republics of Russian Turkestan. The whole of Azarbaijan was theirs, the Soviet republic so called as well as the Persian, and, on the east, they held Tukharistan, now occupied in part by the kingdom of Afghanistan. Over this vast area the king of kings reigned with an effectiveness which varied according to the extent that he could control the satraps, or governors, to whom he deputed authority over the large territories. It was in this great stretch of land that the Iranian language in one form or another was in general predominant, so that it was here that Persian writing for long had its main public.

The language of official communications in the Sasanian period, which was brought to an end by the irruption of the Muḥammadan Arabs into Persia just before the middle of the seventh century, is known to us as Pehlevi. This is sometimes called "Middle" Persian, to distinguish it on the one hand from "Old" Persian, the language of the cuneiform inscriptions of Darius and his successors, and on the other hand from "Modern" or "Islamic" Persian. Islamic Persian, which is a modified form of Pehlevi with a large element of Arabic words in its vocabulary, arose as a practical means of everyday communication after the Muhammadan Arab overrunning of Iran. It is with writings composed in Islamic Persian that we are concerned.

Although in essence the literature of a people is only the sum of individual contributions made over a period of time, yet it reflects the general attitude towards life and its problems and reveals something of the stage of civilization attained by the thinking and writing members of that people. In a measure that attitude is conditioned by the physical, climatic, and geographical circumstances

2

of the territory occupied, circumstances which formed an important factor in the people's economic and political life. Persia's geographical shape is roughly that of a great rim of mountains enclosing vast tracts of plain that is often desert. In the northern regions the winters are severe, and in the summer the heat is moderated by the altitude, whereas along the Persian Gulf summer temperatures are amongst the highest on earth. Except along the Gulf and on the mountain slopes going down to the Caspian Sea, the air is dry and invigorating, rainfall being in general scanty.

Rivers are few and not all have an outlet to the sea, so that human agglomerations are widely distributed, often being found on the slopes of mountains, whose winter snows are husbanded to provide the necessary water, sometimes in very precarious supply. On the richer plains of Azarbaijan, and other areas where water is adequate, grain is cultivated. Almost everywhere mountain tribes rear herds of small cattle whose pastoral requirements, necessitating seasonal migrations, condition the lives of their owners. As for fruits, Persia from the earliest times is known to have produced them in great quantity and variety.

Although it is hardly possible to be out of sight of mountains in Persia, they have never been a serious barrier to communication with her neighbors. Traffic to and from has been constant, whether for war or trade, so that like the people of all civilized nations the Persians are of mixed origin, numbering Iranians, Greeks, Arabs, Turks, and others among their ancestors. The great routes of international commerce linking China, Central Asia, and the Mediterranean were long under Iranian control, as were the sea routes between India and the East African coast. In this traffic, the Zoroastrian, Buddhist, Christian, and Jewish merchants domiciled

3

in Iran had their share, their activities inevitably leading to the import and export of ideas as well as of merchandise.

THE ACHAEMENIAN DYNASTY

The Persians began to figure prominently in world history sometime before the middle of the sixth century B.C., when Cyrus, a descendant of Achaemenes, emerged from his little kingdom of Anshan in southwest Persia and overthrew both Media and Babylon "the Mighty." From his small beginnings he built up for himself a great and famous empire that extended from Grecian Ionia on the Mediterranean Sea away to the lands north and east of the Oxus River in Central Asia. His son and successor Cambyses added the land of Egypt as far south as the First Cataract and Nubia, although troubles developed in the empire after his death.

Darius, who came to the throne after Cambyses, traced his origin through a different branch of the Achaemenid family. After confirming his power, he set about quelling the unruly vassals who had made themselves independent in various parts of the unwieldy and brittle empire. His triumphs over them he commemorated in a long and elaborate inscription engraved in the three languages of his empire, Old Persian, Elamite, and Babylonian. To accommodate it he cleared a wide surface high up on the rock on a side of Behistun mountain, at the foot of which runs the ancient highway connecting the East Mediterranean seaboard with Babylonia and Central Asia. The inscription, begun in 514 B.C., contains one of the earliest pieces of connected prose extant in the language of Iran. Yet it hardly ranks as literature, being not much more than a catalogue of the Great King's military exploits during his campaigns to reduce his treacherous subordinates to order.

4

The script used in all three versions of the manifest was cuneiform, which employed wedge-shaped signs in a variety of combinations to compose syllables and words. It was the established script for royal proclamations and for monuments set up throughout the Achaemenid empire, but its use was restricted and it disappeared with the empire. The story of its decipherment is one of the romances of philological discovery. In 1802, the German scholar Grotefend, while scrutinizing the engraved markings, which had for long been regarded as no more than ornamental designs, found the key to their riddle by identifying the signs used for the names of the Achaemenid potentates Hystaspes, Darius, and Xerxes. His work was followed up and virtually completed by the English traveler Sir Henry Rawlinson, who in 1846 published a translation of the document.

As has been noted, the cuneiform script was of restricted use. For commercial correspondence and royal communications throughout the various provinces of the empire the language conventionally employed was Aramaic, as is known from passages in the Old Testament and from papyri of the fifth century B.C. discovered at Elephantine in Upper Egypt. It was the language of the royal chancellery, and Darius is declared to have sent abroad an Aramaic version of his Behistun proclamation.

Long after the Achaemenids had disappeared from the scene, during the periods when Iran was ruled by the Seleucids, successors of Alexander the Great, and by the Parthian warriors, the use of Aramaic persisted for political purposes among the close corporation of scribes. In a peculiar form—the alphabet only and not the language itself—it survived during the reign of the native Persian dynasty of the Sasanians (224–651). Pehlevi (i.e., Parthavi or "Parthian"), as this kind of script was called, provided an Aramaic cover for Persian words.

Roughly this meant that documents apparently written in Aramaic were in fact in Persian, the characters containing ideograms of Persian words. The script was Aramaic, while vocabulary, construction, and syntax were Persian. Thus the Aramaic words *malkōn malkā* were interpreted and actually read as *shāhan shāh*, the Persian for "king of kings," and *yemallelun-d* was read as *gōvend* ("they say"). In a very restricted way a similar thing occurs in English when the abbreviation "viz." is interpreted as "namely" or "i.e." as "that is." This mode of writing Persian survived the Islamic conquest by a number of centuries and was not entirely displaced by the Arabic of the Muslims, for the sacred books of the Zoroastrians were reproduced in it, a tradition preserved to this day by the Parsi community of India.

The original language of the Avesta, the Zoroastrian scriptures, had its own script, which was not related to the cuneiform of the Achaemenid inscriptions, although the two languages were cognate. How far back the history of Zoroastrianism can be traced is a matter of dispute. Darius, in his Behistun inscription and in others elsewhere, acknowledges the aid granted him by Ahura Mazda, the divine spirit of God. Since Ahura Mazda is a prime figure in the Zoroastrian pantheon, it is assumed that the Achaemenids were followers of the religion established, or represented afresh, by the prophet and reformer Zardusht or Zoroaster, who probably lived in eastern Iran in the seventh century B.C.

What has survived of the Zoroastrian scriptures seems to be only a small part of the original, including the *Gathas* or "hymns" that are ascribed to the founder of the religion and were preserved because they were adapted for ritual purposes. They seem originally to have been sermons in metrical form. For the non-Zoroastrian their interest lies in their profound religious feeling and lofty

6

ethical standards rather than in their attractiveness as literature or their poetic beauty. As for the prose books of the Avesta, they can be likened to the ritual portions of the biblical Book of Leviticus.

THE SASANIAN PERIOD

Religious books formed the bulk of works written down during the reign of the Sasanian shahs, but secular literature in the form of histories, manuals of practical philosophy, and collections of fables embodying ethical maxims also had their place. In the early seventh century the Sasanians came sharply into conflict with their ancient rivals the Greeks in a struggle to secure the mastership of the known world. Each power in turn marched across the lands surrounding the eastern Mediterranean, the victory falling now to one side, now to the other. In 620 the Persians got the upper hand, their empire at that time extending south and west through the efforts of Shahanshah Chosroes Parwiz (590–628). He had succeeded in the preceding fifteen years in driving the Byzantines out of all their possessions in Asia and eastern Africa and had only been prevented from capturing Byzantium itself by the lack of an efficient fleet.

During the years of conflict, however, there had come to power in the eastern Roman Empire the emperor Heraclius, a man well trained in the arts of war. He set to work vigorously to strengthen and reequip his troops and having got them to a stage where he regarded them as fit for war, he attacked the Persians and, in battle after battle, while he himself maintained close touch with his base, drove them to retreat until they had been forced back to Ctesiphon, their capital on the Tigris. Why he did not bring about its capitulation has never been explained. Chosroes, for his part, took advantage of the respite merely to round upon his generals for his past defeats, and paid for his diplomatic error by being assassinated (A.D. 628).

His successor had barely had time to get accustomed to the throne when the province of Iraq was engulfed by disastrous floods. The Tigris and Euphrates had burst their banks simultaneously, and the pestilence which broke out as a result carried off the new shahanshah as one of its victims. From that time onwards the stricken empire was ruled by assassins or puppet sovereigns, who occupied the throne for brief spells, sometimes contemporaneously. In the space of four years no fewer than twelve persons, two of them women, were elevated to power, until, in the words of Gibbon, "every province and almost each city of Persia [became] the scene of independence, of discord, and of bloodshed."

The empire had been overstrained by the warlike Sasanians, and it had cracked. With the material resources of the country wasted by the excessive demands of the Byzantine wars, the people had been driven into a desperate state of poverty, anarchy reigned among the upper classes as well as in the royal house itself, and there was dissatisfaction with the priests of Zoroastrianism. This was the national religion, whose priesthood, "a state within the state," formed a powerful group standing close to the throne. They had looked first to their own interests and cared even less for the spiritual welfare of the people than for their material needs. There had consequently been a decided stirring of revolt against their claim to authority amongst men in their flock with higher ideals, and it had taken the guise, as often, of political unrest. All this, combined with pressure from outside, led to a condition of perilous weakness within the country.

As a state, Iran in fact ceased to exist with the fall of the Sasanians. Yet in the course of their career the

Sasanians had earned for themselves a reputation for good government and expert rulership that was remembered for a century or more after their fall. When the Abbasid caliphs came to power in Baghdad, they modeled their court etiquette and ceremonial and their system of administration upon the Sasanian pattern.

Islamic sentiment, however, with its insistence on the equality of believers before the law, would not have tolerated the class divisions which existed in Iran in Sasanian times, when the Magian code of the Zoroastrians prevailed. This code recognized the king as the supreme head of the state, with four groups under him that were almost castes in the rigidity of their segregation from each other. First came the Magian priests and men holding high political office. Next was the warrior class and, third, the bureaucracy or secretariat that included, in addition to the writers and composers of official correspondence and records, men of education who had acquired special qualifications and could be described as physicians, astrologers, poets, or members of other learned professions. In the fourth group were the manual workers—tillers of the soil, herdsmen, and traders—most degraded of all being the men engaged in occupations that the Zoroastrian priests regarded as polluters of the elements and hence unclean.

Parallel to the grouping of the people, the land itself was divided formally into four great provinces, each under the control of a *marzuban*, "marquis" or "lord of the marches and frontiers." Until well on in the Sasanian era these great territorial princes were paramount in their own areas, although they paid lip service to the shahanshah's overlordship. They stood to him in a kind of feudal relationship, being granted formal possession of their lands in return for their provision of men and materials when the nation was at war and

9

men for the royal bodyguard at other times. They also had to contribute to the revenues required by the state.

The actual collection of materials and money for the royal and provincial treasuries was carried out by a class of hereditary nobles known as *dihqans*, who might be possessed of great estates or of no more property than they carried on their backs, but yet had local knowledge and authority.

It was they, as shall be seen later, who were entrusted with the assessment and collection of revenues by the conquering Muslims. These, being Arab desert-dwellers and nomads, cared nothing for the land and its cultivation, whereas the Zoroastrians had encouraged agriculture and cattle-rearing, which provided the Sasanians with their principal revenues. It was therefore to the interest of the Magian priesthood to prevent exploitation of the peasantry by the *dihqans*, the agents of the central government. When their exactions became too harsh to bear, it frequently happened that villages were deserted by the inhabitants, who migrated to the towns, where they could gather together for protection. It was in fact the growing strength of the towns as centers of handicrafts and commerce that in the long run led to the decline of the serf system and the enfeeblement of the overlords, much as happened in the lands of the West at about the same period.

With the growth of the towns there was associated a growth of skepticism and a decrease in the influence of the Zoroastrian priesthood. This hierarchy formed, in its own estimation, the highest class of the community, but, as has been indicated, it had lost touch with the humbler members of the flock. Early in the Sasanian period there had arisen in the Iraq province a reformer named Mani, who, under the auspices of Shah Shahpur (Sapor I, A.D.

241–272), preached a revised form of the Zoroastrian doctrines. His teaching was based on the well-established Persian concept of the existence of two essential but opposing principles in the universe, the one being light and spirit as represented by Ahura Mazda, and the other darkness and matter represented by Ahriman. Mani might have created little stir if Manichaeism, by which name his religion came to be known, had not also included the doctrine that he was himself the Paraclete, the intercessor for mankind, whose salvation was to be found not in the rites of slaughtering victims for sacrifice, but in prayer and a true comprehension of the universe. Official Magianism denounced the new doctrine as heresy, and removed the danger of Mani by having him executed. It is worthy of note that Manichaeism found a considerable following in Europe, where its teachings also came into conflict with those of the official religion and led to the massacre of its adherents.

Three centuries or so after Mani another reformer appeared in the person of Mazdak. His chief innovation was a demand for equality among all the classes. The prevailing system, by which the few had much and the many had to be content with very little, in his view contained the germs of strife, and he therefore proposed a social reform which would permit all goods, including wives, to be held in common. Only thus, he said, could mankind attain the objective which Zoroastrianism had set up as its goal, namely the defeat of the powers of darkness and the triumph of the spirit of light. His plan was designed to have wide appeal, and this it continued to exert long after the Muhammadans had subordinated Persia. His supporters rebelled periodically in support of his doctrines, but Islam too had views of how society should be organized, and, being possessed of the necessary force, it was able to discomfit the heresy.

THE MUSLIM ARAB INVASION

It was while Iran was in its perilous state of exhaustion that a fresh danger appeared from an unguarded point of the horizon. Its impact when it came was tremendous. Burning with the new and vigorously propagated religion revealed by Muhammad the Apostle of Allah, but with their eyes steadily fixed on the immense riches about which travelers had told them, Arab tribal armies overran the province of Iraq and by A.D. 638 were masters of the Sasanian capital of Seleucia-Ctesiphon on the Tigris. While the main body continued the advance from there over the Zagros range by the ancient highway leading to Khurasan and central Asia, another force, with its base on the island of Bahrain, sailed across the Persian Gulf to invade Khuzistan, the province in which lie the main Persian oil fields of today. Once it was in their hands the way lay open into Fars, the heart of the land.

The Sasanian army took its stand against the main body of the Arabs coming up the Khurasan highway, and the "battle of battles" was fought at Nihawand, about forty miles southwest of Hamadan. On the one side was the largely unorganized Iranian army made up of conscripts, the last gleanings from every province of the Sasanian empire, and on the other the fierce Muslim hordes alive with anticipation of the joys of Paradise if they died as martyrs fighting for Islam, or of equally desirable rewards if they survived to overrun the, to them, fabulously wealthy land of Persia. Already their appetites had been sharpened by a series of victories. Nihawand was just another triumph to add to the list. The Iranian king, Yazdigard III, escaped from the wreckage of his army leaving the national palladium, the leathern apron of the hero Kaveh the Blacksmith, in the hands of the Arabs. Even had the Persians fought with all the courage they had displayed in the wars against Byzantium, the result would probably not have been greatly different. The knights who formed the core of their battle array were heavily armored and slow moving, whereas the Arabs were trained in nimble skirmishing. Most were armed only with bows and arrows, but they appear also to have acquired mangonels and other engines of war from the Greeks with whom they had been in contact, and undoubtedly they were reinforced by fellow Arabs who had fought against the Greeks and so learned new forms of strategy and tactics.

After their defeat, not a few of the Persian knights in command of troops came over to be Islamized, taking their men with them. At a later stage of the invasion, as the historian Tabari relates in his account of the siege of Tustar, numbers of such nobles, after secretly making contact with the enemy, returned to the strongholds in which their countrymen were still holding out and surreptitiously admitted the besiegers. As one town after another fell, the Arab military commanders handed over the local administration to the *dihqans* and others who had been in charge during the Sasanian regime. Many, whether Islamized or not, in return for their services got a share of the booty taken from their own countrymen which the Arabs collected in each town.

Outside the towns, as inside them, while the Arabs kept ultimate control strictly in their own hands, they allowed the *dihqans* to continue in charge of the areas of which they possessed special knowledge, where more often than not they had been the collectors of revenues. The odium they suffered was no doubt due in part to the exactions of the overlords, but tax-farming leads to abuses. In addition, the Arabs in Persia, like invaders everywhere, had to exploit the local inhabitants in order to secure supplies and shelter for themselves and their animals, and to receive services of one kind or another. Grievances were inevitable.

There was little prospect for rank-and-file Arabs to return home to their deserts even if they had wished to do so. Many of them married Persian women and settled in the larger centers, where they gradually merged with the local population and adopted Persian ways of life. They became accustomed to Persian cookery, discarded their loincloths and robes in favor of trousers, and appeared in public to celebrate the Zoroastrian festivals of Nauruz in the spring and Mihrgan in the autumn. Coming from a land at a fairly simple stage of civilization, where they had been either nomadic desert-dwellers or inhabitants of small towns, they were transported with little preparation to a country which had a long-established social system, flourishing commerce, and every evidence of luxurious living. It is not to be wondered at that even the most sophisticated of them were impressed, and that the historians have transmitted long and circumstantial accounts of the treasures that were sent back to Arabia for distribution by the caliph.

Between Persians of the upper class and the Arab military leaders relations were not always as cordial as among the rank and file, even when the adoption of Islam might have been expected to heighten cordiality. It is true that no severe pressure had been put upon the Persians to adopt the new faith, and that the Arabs, having no tradition of government at home, were glad to make use of the experience of the conquered people. But, especially under the regime of the Umayyad caliphs of Damascus, the Arab leaders adopted an arrogant tone of superiority, treating the Persian "free men," even after adoption of Islam, as inferiors and extorting state taxes even though, as happened in Iraq, they allowed the owners to retain their lands. The Umayyad sheiks in fact did

14

not hesitate to proclaim that henceforth it was they who would form the privileged class in Persia. Power was on their side.

The Persians for their part made a show of submission but clung to their accustomed ways of life. This may explain how they managed to retain the language they spoke basically unchanged, whereas other peoples, such as the Syrians, the Egyptians, the North Africans, and for a time many of the people of Spain, surrendered their mother tongues in favor of Arabic. Even in Persia, because it was the language of the Prophet and of the Koran, Arabic was venerated by Muslims and thus became the language of theology, science, and serious literature generally, until national sentiment made the use of Persian desirable and practicable. Although Arabic was the language of government and administration, the *dihqans* continued the use of the Sasanian tax registers, which were naturally in Pehlevi, for a considerable period after the invasion. But the change to Arabic was inevitable. An intermediate stage is to be seen in the Muhammadan coins bearing both Arabic and Pehlevi legends which were struck on the Sasanian model by the new Arab governors of the Persian provinces. In Bukhara such coins continued to be struck until well on in the Abbasid period, the practice being finally ended about the end of the second century of the Hegira, A.D. 815.

It should here be noted that the earliest specimens of written Persian were not set down in the Arabic script. Amongst them are some in the Manichaean characters derived from Syriac, while an inscription discovered in Afghanistan, and bearing a date of the Seleucid era corresponding to A.D. 752–753, is in Hebrew characters. As elsewhere in the Orient, the alphabet employed by the writer of a document is usually an indication of his religion, and so it is that as Islam advanced the Arabic

15

script came more commonly into use, although it was not until about the end of the third century of the Hegira (the ninth century after Christ) that the Arabic form of writing can be held to have displaced the Middle Persian style. It had taken all that time to Islamize the country, for, away from the main highways, mountains and deserts hindered military advance, and in the remoter provinces such as Sistan and out-of-the-way parts of Bukhara and the southern Caspian shores indigenous cultures kept tenacious hold upon local rulers and *dihqans*.

Obviously the first of the population who found it to their interest to accept the new faith were the captives taken in battle, who were in any event not likely to have been given much choice. As has been seen, there was here and there dissatisfaction with Magianism and it was no great matter to the mass of the people to substitute Allah for Ahura Mazda, the principle of good and light, and Shaitan or Iblis (the Devil) for Ahriman, the principle of evil and darkness. The ritual demands made of converts at that early stage were of the simplest. All they were told was: "If you will worship as we worship and eat of our slaughtering, then you are Muslims." When Muslims seized a town, they encountered no strong opposition from the inhabitants and were in fact welcomed by that class of workers who earned their living by trades regarded as defiling the sacred elements of fire or water.

Across the Oxus the invaders found progress more difficult amongst the people, many of whom were Buddhists and not at once persuaded that Islam was to their spirtual advantage. At Bukhara the year 94 of the Hegira, corresponding to A.D. 712–713, the victorious Umayyad general Qutaibah ibn Muslim turned what had been a Buddhist temple into a mosque, to which the inhabitants were summoned by public criers every Friday.

But attendance appears not to have been obligatory, because a reward of two dirhems was held out as an inducement to worshipers. The congregation was drilled in the ritual of worship by a man who stood at the back calling out to newly introduced believers when they were to bow and when to cease bowing, when they were to prostrate themselves and when to rise, and so forth. In those early days the Koran was recited in Persian at the Friday services in the mosque, since Arabic was not as yet commonly familiar.

In Persia proper Islam overlaid rather than destroyed the feeling of coherence in the people and their loyalty to their country. This displayed itself, even as the new religion spread, in their adopting a special attitude towards it, resulting in Shiism. The Prophet Muhammad had died in the year 632 leaving no heir and without indicating who should succeed him. He had declared in the Koran that he was the "Seal," that is "the Concluding Link," in the long line of prophets which he regarded as having began with Adam, the first man. To the extent that there could have been no Apostle of Allah after him, he was justified. There was, however, the new and rapidly growing Islamic state for which a head had to be found in succession to himself.

After some debate the Islamic community at Medina, the capital, selected Muhammad's father-in-law Abu Bakr to be his *khalifah* (caliph), i.e., "successor" or "substitute." He was followed after his death by Omar, a man of strong character who, in addition to becoming caliph, assumed or was given the title of "commander of the faithful." Realizing the difficulties that might follow his own demise and to ensure that the succession to his office would not be left to chance, he nominated a council of six who were to elect the next caliph. When in due course they elected Uthman, member of the sheikly family of Umayyads that afterward supplied a line of caliphs, they passed over a candidate who, in the opinion of a large number of the faithful, had a far better right to the caliphate than anyone else. This was Ali, cousin and son-in-law of the Prophet, whose rejection brought about a drastic cleavage in the Muslim community that was not healed even when, ultimately, Uthman was assassinated and Ali became the fourth of the "orthodox" caliphs, as they were called.

Resenting the election, an Umayyad sheik set himself up in a rival caliphate at Damascus in Syria, and there founded a dynasty by the device of securing the succession to his own son and members of his family. This step offended two kinds of Muslims, first those who held that the principles of the faith demanded freedom of election to the caliphate, and second, especially in Persia and its one-time province of Iraq, those who held that only a son of Ali, who was in the direct line of succession to the Prophet, could legitimately be the imam, or leader, of Islam. Of the sons of Ali, one was Husain, whose mother was the Prophet's daughter Fatimah and whose wife was a daughter of Yazdigard, the last Sasanian king. He thus had a special claim on Persian sympathies.

Opposition to the Umayyad pretensions culminated in war, in which the last battle took place at Kerbela, situated not far from the ancient Babylon. There the Umayyad troops had little difficulty in routing the meager forces of Husain, who himself found death as a martyr. The event brought a wave of sympathy for the Alid cause and led to the formation of the *Shi'a* or "party," of Ali, which played an important part in the subsequent religious and political history of Islam. The tragedy of Kerbela is universally commemorated amongst the Shiites in every Muslim country as a day of mourning, and adherents of the Alid cause have in general kept themselves aloof from the main body of Muslims, namely, those who have called themselves *Sunnis*, followers of the *Sunnah*, or "Tradition."

THE ABBASID CALIPHS

To the Umayyads Kerbela was only an incident in a long campaign. They continued their penetration of Iran and for ninety years dominated the land, where their autocratic methods at last stirred a growing antipathy into active revolt. Disaffection centered in Merv, a large city in Khurasan, which province, remote from the capital at Damascus, was one where Iranian national sentiment had been kept strongly alive. Here were set up the head-quarters of a secret campaign to destroy the reigning caliphate and substitute a certain Abu'l-Abbas, a kinsman of the Prophet through descent from the latter's uncle Abbas. The chief of the Abbasid propagandists cunningly adopted as his battle cry "The House of Hashim," Hashim having been the common ancestor both of the Alids and of Abbas, and so induced those favoring the Alid claim to give him their support. It was Abu'l-Abbas, however, who, in 750, was proclaimed caliph, thus shattering the hopes of the Alids.

To secure their own position the Abbasid supporters had massacred a large number of the Umayyad family. The Abbasid victory ended Arab claims to superiority within the Muslim community, those who gained the most politically from the change being the Khurasanis. In 762 the Abbasids founded their new capital of Baghdad near the old Sasanian capital of Ctesiphon. There for more than three-quarters of a century they reigned in splendor, acknowledging the assistance they had derived from Persia, and more especially from Khurasan, by appointing Persians to high office in the state. Amongst these were the famous Barmecide (Barmakid) family, three generations of whom served the early Abbasids as viziers for half a century (752–804). Their ancestors had been high priests of the great Magian fire temple at Balkh (Baktria), but as Muslims they themselves were faithful servants of the state, until Caliph Harun al-Rashid in a fit of jealous suspicion of their ever-growing influence destroyed the whole family, whose vast riches automatically passed into his own treasury. As long, however, as the great figures of the Abbasid dynasty held the reins of the caliphate, Persians were to be found in positions of high office under them.

Once the outstanding caliphs had passed from the scene there came a period of rapid decline, when the harem-bred weaklings who succeeded fell to hiring Turcoman palace guards to protect them. In the hands of these fierce warriors the head of Islam became no more than a lever for furthering their own ambitions, a fact which could not long be concealed from shrewd watchers beyond the palace walls. In Persia his lieutenants seized on the fact that the caliph no longer ruled and were quick to take advantage of the situation. The Abbasid victory marked the first great rift in the Muslim empire. Now came another. Iran broke into pieces, each with its master, who maintained only very tenuous links with the caliphate.

The original Arab invasion had overlaid the civilization of Persia with a silt which had at first covered it up in varying depths. Under the surface, however, it continued to grow and was stirred to fresh life by the fertile vigor of the conquerors. Development was not everywhere uniform and the results were not obvious until more than a century and a half had gone by. Then, very early in the third century of Islam, local patriotism, after the process of hardening under Umayyad arrogance, received an extra impetus, which attained great force when the

Abbasids began their decline. It was not concentrated in any one center, but it appeared first in provinces like Khurasan remote from the capital of the caliphate. In that province lay the great trading city of Balkh, which was rich and populous, the political and commercial center of a huge area. Its language came to be known as *Farsi Dari* (Court Persian), and it was mostly here that there developed the language of Persian literature as we know it.

The political severance from the caliphate as the culmination of national rebirth was naturally accompanied by the gradual restoration of the Persian tongue in the new form enriched by Arabic, as a language which might be used for works of literature. For theology and the sciences Arabic retained its preeminence, while for works associated with the cult of Zoroastrianism Pehlevi continued in active use for two centuries after the first Muslim onslaught on Iran, being known and studied for three more centuries after that. Scholars and men of letters in the Umayyad and early Abbasid days had continued to expound the contents of the Pehlevi classics that had survived the Arab invasion, or been composed after it, and made them known to their fellow countrymen by translating them into Arabic. Easily the most famous of the translators was a convert from Magianism who, on becoming a Muslim, had adopted the name of Ibn al-Muqaffa'. Most of his life was spent at Basra and, in the course of his literary activities, he turned from their original Pehlevi into Arabic first the book of animal fables that came to be known as *Kalila va Dimna* and then the "Book of Kings." This latter work provided the tenth-century epic writer Firdausi with the materials for his vast *Shahnama*, but it was also a source for various Arabic histories that described the Sasanian and earlier monarchies of Iran.

With the political independence of the country practically achieved, the Persian tongue was coming into its own alongside Arabic as the idiom of literature. At first this variety of Persian had to be learned by its users as an addition to their mother dialects, and it was at the courts of the rulers who had shaken off the Arab temporal power that the poets of Iran began to experiment with their newly acquired medium. There it was molded and polished into an elegant instrument for the recording of ideas and emotions, by the very men who were adapting the Arabic language itself to the needs of Muslim theology and science in the wider sense. The men of the desert had had few abstract concepts to deal with in their mode of life and hence had not felt the need of words with which to formulate and discuss them. Although the vocabulary of Zoroastrianism had a few equivalents in Arabic, they had to be supplemented, and Islam in addition introduced fresh institutions and ideas, with a new terminology. Scholarly Persians therefore set about the task of evolving and elaborating from existing Arabic roots the words demanded by the new learning, thereby turning both Arabic and Persian, not to mention other Islamic languages, into flexible and powerful media of expression for the scientist, the philosopher, and the theologian.

The connection between the beginnings of Islamic-Persian poetry and prose and the political circumstances which fostered them is not accidental. Normally, "pure" poetry or artistic prose is the expression of the author's personal reaction to his immediate environment or to his own emotional experiences, which he can, if he has the necessary skill, impart to other human beings and find them echoed there. That kind of poetry is certainly contained in the *divans*, or collected works, of the Persian versifiers, but the best was to be found only after a period

22

of development had gone by. In the early stages, poetry in Iran was written for specific motives engendered by the circumstances of the independent courts that came into being with the decline of the Abbasids, and whose rise to power requires some digression into political history.

THE RISE OF PERSIAN PRINCES

In 820 Caliph Mamun, son of Harun al-Rashid and one of the most powerful and enlightened of the Abbasids, had entrusted the viceroyalty of the province of Khurasan to his general Tahir Dhu'l-Yaminain (possessor of the two felicitous stars), a man of Persian stock. After about a year and a half of vassalship, this ambitious soldier made a bid for independence, disclosing his intention one Friday by omitting Mamun's name from the prayer in which the caliph's title was normally mentioned as token of his suzerainty. But Tahir had mistaken the kind of man he was dealing with, and he died that same night. His son Talha, who had previously been nominated as his successor, submitted to Mamun and was confirmed in the viceroyalty, an office in which he was succeeded in his turn by his brother Abd Allah. The retention of so important a post in the hands of successive members of the same family speaks to their strength and influence in the province, from which even Mamun did not venture to oust them, in spite of Tahir's original defection.

The new viceroy was faced by numerous domestic troubles, not only because of constant outbreaks from religio-political rebels, collectively known as *Kharijis* (secessionists), but also because of incessant disputes in the agricultural communities over water rights, a matter of prime importance in areas where rainfall is scanty. He proved equal to the situation, reducing the rebels by military action and dealing with the irrigation disputes

23

by convening a committee of legists from Khurasan and Iraq to draw up a code governing the distribution of water. After his death the amirate, or command, of Khurasan passed from one member of his family to another, finally coming into the hands of a wastrel, against whom the Caspian province of Tabaristan revolted under the leadership of an Alid warrior. Soon the neighboring province of Jurjan was in rebellion, and there was turmoil over the whole region.

There, circumstances offered chances of profit to any man of initiative and enterprise, and they were seized by a warrior who became famous in Persian history as Ya'qub ibn Laith Saffar, "the Coppersmith." He had begun life in an obscure village in the province of Sistan and, migrating to the capital, learned the trade of a coppersmith, in which he prospered by his enterprise, and became a popular figure. Urban trade, however, provided insufficient scope for his abounding energies, and he left to join a band of guerrilla warriors who financed their charitable and political activities out of the proceeds of robberies on the highway. Chieftainship of the band was only a step to his being offered the post of amir, or commander, of the government forces in Sistan, a position which made him virtual governor of the province. From there into the disturbed areas beyond his boundaries demanded little more than a triumphal march.

A famous and characteristic story is told that when the Coppersmith was approaching Khurasan he was met by an envoy bearing a letter from the caliph's viceroy stationed at Nishapur, then the capital. It read: "If you come by command of the caliph, produce your written authority that I am to hand over the province to you. If not, then turn back." From underneath the prayer rug on which he was seated, the Coppersmith drew a sword. "This," he said, "is my authority."

The Coppersmith knew no Arabic, and when the panegyrists began to acclaim his prowess in Arabic verse, he demanded impatiently to know why they said things he could not understand. He was succeeded by his brother Amr, who came to terms with the caliph and was granted the governship of a huge territory of which Khurasan was only a part. But Amr was not content with this. His eyes strayed to the richer lands beyond the Oxus, into which he attempted a crossing. Their ruler, however, was a member of the powerful family of the Samanids, who overthrew him and sent him in chains to Baghdad.

The Samanids first came into prominence when Saman Khudat, a Magian nobleman, attracted the attention of the Abbasid governor of Khurasan, later to become Caliph Mamun, and accepted Islam at his hands. When the prince departed for Baghdad to assume the caliphate, he left instructions that Saman's son and grandsons were to be well provided for. In due course they became masters of a vast stretch of territory that at one time extended from the frontiers of China at Kashghar as far southwest as Kirmanshah. Parts of this huge area ultimately fell away from them, but the family held firmly to the provinces of Khurasan, Gurgan, Transoxiana, and Tukharistan (the modern Afghanistan) for a long period of their dominance (A.D. 874–999).

Saman, founder of the dynasty, had traced his ancestry back to Bahram Chubin, the warrior who for a time had usurped the throne of the Sasanians, and his descendants, proud of their Iranian origin, did much to encourage a patriotic spirit in their subjects. They always retained friendly relationships with the caliphate, while at the same time asserting their own nationalism. Surrounding themselves with courtiers and men of letters who shared their views, and regarding themselves as in the direct line of succession to the Sasanians, they made great efforts to adhere to old established custom and practice. Towards the latter part of their period they had rivals in parts of Iran not occupied by themselves where rulers independent both of them and of the caliphs held power. But in the fostering of national arts and literature the Samanids took first place.

The presence of a poet at court was an ancient tradition of royalty, an essential part of the pomp and circumstance attaching to it. At the Persian courts he not only occupied himself in celebrating his master's triumphs but also performed a very practical function which corresponds in some measure with that of the press attaché or "public relations officer" of today. The ode, intended to flatter the prince by an elaboration of his noble virtues and magnificent exploits in the field, might serve a secondary purpose by being distributed among rivals as a challenge, among potential usurpers as a warning, and among the general population subject to the prince as a manifesto of his greatness.

The poet himself benefited in more than one way. If his master was generously inclined and the panegyric satisfactorily rich in flattery, the composer might be rewarded with a mouthful of jewels, a splendidly caparisoned horse, or a lovely slave girl. Copies might be sent to neighboring courts, there to gain fresh laurels for him and to provide him with alternative markets for his wares should the first patron fail to provide rewards that came up to expectation, or lose interest after a while. It was not unknown for a poet to hawk his compositions about from one court to another, changing a name here and a line there as circumstances made expedient. Understandably a ready pen could turn from praise to abuse. There was no lack of people who would be willing to hire him—or to buy him off, if necessity arose.

TWO : THE FORMS OF
PERSIAN VERSE

The older and more traditional Persian critics and literary historians have generally given preference to "linked" speech, or verse, over prose, or "dispersed" speech. One reason may have been that verse, with its lines established by meter and rhyme, provided a succession of self-contained propositions or sentences, and at a time when literary work was almost a matter of improvisation, or when author or rhapsodist recited aloud from memory, the two elements of meter and rhyme were of great assistance to composition. Prose, on the other hand, without aid from these elements and with no system of punctuation or capital letters to indicate where one sentence ended and another began, was a matter of some difficulty.

QASIDA AND CHANSON

For that reason, probably, the earliest as well as the most numerous specimens of literary Persian that we possess are in verse, generally in the *qasida* form. For its theme, the qasida in the ordinary course had some eulogistic, often grossly flattering, things to say about a patron, who would be expected to pay for the service rendered. It was when Persian princes made themselves independent of the Baghdad caliphate and set up courts for themselves that the qasida became a common form and Persian poets began to reap rewards for composing verse in their own tongue. In its beginnings Muslim Persian literature was aristocratic in outlook, in the same way that pre-Muslim literature had been. Clearly the people at large, whether peasants or city-dwellers, must have had their own entertainers, with stories, ballads, and tunes that had a special appeal for them. Between them and the members of the princely courts there was a well-defined cleavage and Persia was, and for long remained, a class-conscious country. The native essayists who deal with literature and music give clear instructions to the practitioners about what is suited to each class of the community.

They show that the court of the Sasanian shah was always the resort of people who could provide the shah with entertainment as well as with instruction. Jesters and clowns were amongst them, but all had to be persons of unblemished physique and character who, moreover, could boast of good birth. It was said that no one was admitted into the royal presence whose father had followed a mean occupation, such as weaving or cupping, even though the candidate for admission was learned in all the mysteries and master of all the sciences. The requirements at the Muhammadan courts were probably not so strict. It was the ambition of most poets to secure a footing at some princely court, where he could mingle with senior practitioners in his art and gather hints on how to work to the best effect. His prime object, as an essayist of the eleventh century expressed it, was to establish a reputation, "to be recited by the tongues of free men, to have his work transcribed in albums, and to be quoted in cities." Only then would he have attained the capacity to immortalize his patron.

The chosen form for the panegyric, as has been said, was the qasida. Its composition was a craft regarded by the poets themselves as requiring technical training quite as much as native endowment. To them it was a trade like jewelry manufacture or even carpentry, a skill to be acquired by apprenticeship and experience. Accordingly the textbooks of prosody give the novice instruction in the mechanics of his business, telling him he must begin by committing to memory the good things of the masters, and then analyze their linguistic devices, all the time familiarizing himself with the conventions of the poetic art, which must always be strictly followed. "Studio" training was important. It consisted of putting down the theme of a prospective ode in prose, considering what style of language was appropriate, deciding on the right meter, and finally writing all down in verse form.

It was not open to the poet to choose the framework of his theme, for the qasida was composed on a set pattern, with a fixed type of rhyme. It might contain almost any number of lines, of which twelve was the usual minimum, though many were far longer, each line being in two balanced halves corresponding to each other in meter and parallel in theme. The two halves of the opening line rhymed together, all the remaining lines at the end repeating the rhyme of the first. To compose a qasida was a test of the poet's skill in the adaptation of meter to theme and of his ingenuity in rhyming.

Transferring these rigid features from one language to another is a matter of the utmost difficulty. Yet the Arabic qasida form appears to have been taken over not only by the Persian poets but also by the troubadours and jongleurs of Provence, whose *chansons* bear a striking resemblance in structure to that of the Arabic and Persian qasidas. The chanson, as its name indicates, was originally meant to be sung or recited, and not just scanned by the eyes of a reader in a book. Such was the case initially with all kinds of literature, including the qasida and its offshoot the *ghazal*, for the composition of which the Persian word used is *saraidan* (to sing) and, since they were meant to be heard, they contained repetitions and stock phrases that would be acceptable to the ear though probably wearisome to a reader's eye. Both are also in monorhyme, however long the poem. English with its poverty of rhyming words and rhyming grammatical affixes is ill adapted to illustrate form, but the following translation of the introductory part of a chanson may convey some impression of the rhyming scheme:

> A king who wears our France's crown of gold
> Worthy must be, and of his body bold;
> That man soe'er to him do evil wold [would],
> He may not quit in any manner hold
> Till he be dead or to his mercy yold [yield].
> Else France shall lose her praise she hath of old.
> Falsely he's crowned; so hath our story told.[1]

By the time the qasida form became common in Iran, it was falling into disuse in the place of its origin, the Arabian desert. There it had opened with an erotic prelude, the poet's lament that having come to a rendez-vous to meet his beloved he had found only the cold ashes of her tribe's campfire. Once he had succeeded in arousing the emotional interest of his audience, he turned to the real purpose (*qasida* means *purpose*) of his poem, which might be a eulogy on a patron, a paean of victory, a

[1] G. Saintsbury, *The Flourishing of Romance* (Edinburgh, 1897).

description of the springtime or of the animals peopling the desert, an elegy or an abusive attack on a rival poet. Most frequently of all it was a panegyric, as we have seen. To town-dwellers, even in Arabia, the desert had small reality and was regarded as the stereotyped setting for whatever subject the author had in mind. In Persia almost everywhere it was, from the time of its arrival, a purely artificial framework for the poet's real theme, which might be as varied as in the Arabic counterpart.

It has been said above that the qasida was sung or recited. If the poet lacked the voice or the presence, or perhaps the self-confidence, necessary for a public presentation of his work, he employed a *ravi*, or rhapsodist, to sing it for him. The link between poet and *ravi* corresponded closely with that between the troubadour or *trouveur*, who was the author, and the jongleur, who was the public performer. The *ravi*, like the latter, often had a large repertory made up of verses by a number of different poets, to which he might very well add some of his own composition. What has survived of Persian poetry consists of the materials orally transmitted by *ravis* (who might be either men or women), and finally put into writing, as a general rule long after the death of the original authors. The choice of themes was strictly defined by tradition and as many authors might use the same ones, it is never sure, in view of the notoriously treacherous character of the human memory, that what is contained in the reputed *divans*, or collected works, of poets is necessarily attributable to the "onlie true begetter."

It is nevertheless possible, from what has come down to us, to judge the nature of the contents of the qasida and the uses to which it was adapted. The chief of these, then, was the panegyric or eulogy, very often composed in a most exaggerated, sometimes ludicrous, bombastic style. An idea of the lengths to which an author could go

in flattery of a patron may be gathered from the following
introduction to a qasida by the recognized master of the
form, Anvari, who, toward the end of his life (*ca.* 1190)
repented of the base uses to which he had put his very
great poetical skill:

> Thou art far above the skies exalted,
> Thy light is to the world a second sun
> To whom is turned the gaze of all mankind.
> Both great and small regard thee as their choice;
> The humblest threshold of thy royal court
> Out-tops the pinnacle of Heaven's dome.[1]

This specimen of the panegyric art was addressed to a
certain Ala al-Din Muhammad, an obscure person of
whom nothing more is known than his name.

It is difficult for us at this distance of time and space
to understand what pleasure a man, though he might be
newly sprung to wealth and power, could derive from
compliments he could buy for money. This explains why
qasidas of this type have so rarely been translated into
Western tongues and why their authors have been regarded
as insincere and mercenary peddlers of worthless flattery.
The poets themselves were fully conscious of the unworthy
nature of their work, and the critics were always pointing
out the dangers of running into exaggeration in the
qasida. So the author of the *Qabus-nama*, a book of
counsel designed for kings and courtiers in the eleventh
century, warns poets against telling a man who has never
possessed so much as a dagger that his sword "subdues
the lion," or one who has never had the courage even to
mount a donkey, that his horse "is a very Rakhsh or
Shabdiz," both fiery steeds renowned in Persian legend.
Some Persian critics hold it against poetry in general that

---

[1] No attempt is here made to imitate the rhyme or meter of the
original. For scansion of transliterated verse, see Appendix A below.

it concerns itself either with flattery or love, and that both are incentives to falsehood. As one of them phrases it, "Our poets blacken the face of their intelligence with the smoke of greed and dull the eye of their genius with the dust of shamelessness."

From our point of view, it may be said that to be deterred from reading qasidas by the hyperbolic or otherwise repellent features of the contents is, for those who are familiar with Persian, to miss the rhythm of the verse and the pleasure to be derived from skillful use of language. Persian critics themselves are apt to regard the theme as immaterial, looking rather to the form and construction of the verse, with special regard to style, vocabulary, and use of rhyme. Since the subject matter is very often conventional, the form becomes important, so that the good qasida, as Pope said of true wit, is: "Nature to advantage dressed/What oft was thought, but ne'er so well expressed."

GHAZAL AND LYRIC VERSE

A people with as long a cultural tradition as the Iranians, and one endowed with such fertility of imagination, could not be content merely to borrow. As in other fields, they adapted what they took; out of the erotic prelude of the qasida they fashioned the ghazal (a word derived from an Arabic original meaning "lovers' exchanges"), a separate lyric form having something of the character of the European sonnet. So far as rhyme is concerned it follows the qasida in structure, but it is normally much shorter, consisting of about eight to fourteen lines, the last of which at a later stage of development contained the poet's pen name. The framework is fixed, since there was no poetic license, and in each line rhythm and meaning coincide. The contents are lighter than those of the

33

qasida, and the style of language used is more polished. The most normal theme was love, mystical or human, the homosexual being recognized; but anything might be touched on that stirred the emotions—the caprices of fortune's whirligig, the mystery of life in the world, the upsurging happiness of springtime, or the joys and sorrows of friendship or other earthly attachments. Subjects like these touch most human beings, and the spark struck by the poet may leap the gap between man and man.

When verse appears in the musical language of the masters of the ghazal, the thirteenth-century Sa'di of Shiraz and his even greater fellow citizen Hafiz, who lived about a hundred years later, it becomes understandable why Persians have always preferred it to prose for their literary efforts. "Verse is to prose," says the eleventh-century author of the *Qabus-nama*, "as the king is to his subjects, what is suited to one being unsuited to the other." Two centuries later, Shamsi Qais, author of a manual of prosody and the poetic art, being perhaps not altogether disinterested, proclaimed bluntly:

However good your prose may be, it is improved when a poet turns it into stanzas felicitously worded. In poetry the fortunate man expressed his joy on his day of happiness, in poetry the warrior boasts of his victory on the day of battle. And let him who attracts the poet's displeasure beware, for he will never wipe away the stain.

In the opinion of the fifteenth-century literary biographer Daulatshah, "famous poets are the tirewomen who clothe virgin ideas in wedding garb; or they are the divers who bring up the pearls from imagination's depths." In the Persian idiom, a poet deals with verses as though they were pearls which he strings together after he has pierced them. Hafiz, in the closing line of one of his best known ghazals, apostrophizes himself and says:

You've spoken your ode, having strung your pearls,
  Now Hafiz, sing it sweetly to us;
For on your verse the sky has strewn
  Pearls from the necklet of the Pleiades.

Each verse of the ghazal is usually complete in itself, though one meter and a single rhyme run through the whole poem, the second half of each line balancing the first half in theme and echoing it in rhythm. From their being self-contained in this fashion, it is not unusual to find that the lines of a ghazal in one edition are set down in a different order from those in another, giving rise to the criticism that it is difficult to follow any one theme throughout a single ghazal. In modern times the reply to that criticism has been that the lines are in fact variations on a theme, their subtleties being too deep for the ordinary uninitiated hearer or reader. However, one brilliant line can make a ghazal, and establish its author's fame as a poet.

RUBA'I OR QUATRAIN

In the Western world, for a century or more past, the best known form of Persian poetry has been that of the *ruba'i* or quatrain (foursome), made famous by Edward FitzGerald's poem *The Ruba'iyat of Omar Khayyam*. This form was probably an invention of the Persians and consists of an epigram in four half-lines of which the first, second, and fourth rhyme together, while the third is usually outside the rhyming scheme. Within this brief structure a theme is stated and developed, coming to a climax in the last half-line, before which the unrhymed third marks an anticipatory pause. Generally the form gives the impression of something unstudied and spontaneous and at the same time terse, and it is very much something "thrown off" to mark an occasion. There is

35

scarcely a man of letters in the whole galaxy of Persian authors, whatever his subject, who at some period of his life did not compose ruba'iyat. Often they revealed his true feelings rather than his public "face," and for that reason had to be discreetly worded or issued anonymously if they were not to invite serious consequences from political or religious authorities. Normally the language of Sufism was equivocal enough to provide a mode of escape, if need should arise.

Of Khayyam it was said he "unraveled the tangles of metaphysics with the finger tips of the ruba'i," or, in other words, touched upon highly dangerous topics revealing his freedom of thought in veiled idiom. The anonymity associated with the form provided another and even better shield against attack. The form is reputed by the Persian biographers to have been introduced to popular use either by the tenth-century poet Abu Shukur of Balkh or by the Sufi Abu Sa'id, son of Abu'l-Khair, who lived about a century later. Yet, since something very like it has been identified in the *Gathas*, or Zoroastrian hymns, the probability is that it is at least as early as the beginning of the Sasanian period.

Abu Sa'id nevertheless set his mark on the form, used by him for the exposition of mystical pantheism, which he described in fanciful metaphors that became characteristic of its verse. It is well exemplified in the following epigram:

I said, Thou art comely, whose art Thou?
She said, Mine own—I am myself I vow;
  I'm Lover, Love, Beloved all in one;
And Mirror, Beauty, Sight—all's one, I trow.

In another quatrain he reveals the distinction made by Sufism between Reality and the Otherness which constitutes the world of phenomena. It reads:

36

Upbraid me not, master, for indulging in wine,
For acting the lover and worshiping wine.
  In soberness those about me are strangers,
But lost to sense I am at one with the friend.[1]

Here "wine" is the means of divine intoxication and the "friend" the impersonation of divine truth, the one reality. Still another quatrain expresses the same concept:

From Thee I was never parted whilst I remained in being;
Therein lies the proof of my fortunate star.
  If I have ceased to be, into Thine Essence I have vanished;
If I exist, it is by Thy Light that I am apparent.

In the following the poet marks his preference for the inward illumination of Sufism over the formal duties and ritual prescribed by orthodoxy:

The fighter for the faith is ever in pursuit of martyrdom,
Unwitting that love's martyr is far nobler than he.
  On Resurrection Day how shall the two compare,
The one slain by the enemy, the other slain [extinguished] by
        the Friend?

On occasion he is not above using the equivocal language of the Sufis which became so characteristic in the ghazal, where what was to the outward eye a piece of eroticism could be given a transcendental meaning. Thus:

Last night I lay with my loved one, ever gracious to me.
From me came nothing but worship, from her 'twas kindness
        all.
  But e'er our love was told, the night had passed swiftly
        away.
What blame could attach to the night, the tale of our love
        being so long?

[1] It is impossible to convey in English the texture of the Persian verse and, since rhyme always works by the anticipation of the ear, or the eye, there must always be a sense of disappointment where it is lacking in the translation. But it would be improper to alter the spirit of the thought for the sake of meter or rhyme.

During the lifetime of Abu Sa'id there was born the author of the ruba'iyat best known to the Western world, namely Omar-i Khayyam, or "Omar son of the Tent-maker." A native of Nishapur in Khurasan, he became astronomer to Malikshah, one of the Turcoman Seljuq sultans whose warlike activities stirred Europe to the First Crusade. Like most educated Iranians, Omar composed occasional quatrains, but the biographers who record such details as are known of his life ascribe no poetry to him, confining themselves exclusively to his achievements in mathematics and science. Not until certain of Omar's quatrains were woven into a connected poem by Edward FitzGerald, a nineteenth-century English amateur of Persian literature, did it become known in the West that Omar had claims to poetical talent. It was in fact something of a revelation to his countrymen themselves.

There is therefore no accredited divan of Omar Khayyam, and in view of the large stock of "floating" quatrains in existence it would be rash to state categorically which were his. He is generally declared to have lived until the year 1123, but we have no earlier manuscript than one of the fourteenth century mentioning his quatrains, and that quotes only thirteen. In later manuscripts the numbers increase as the dates advance, so that a fairly recent one contains rather more than eight hundred. The fact that literary Persian changed little over the centuries provides an extra hazard on the way to pointing to any quatrain with the assurance of its being his, especially as the themes belong to the traditional stock.

Out of the large number at his disposal FitzGerald picked out those which suited his own thesis, supplementing them at need from the works of Sufi poets. Out of that material he built up for himself a picture of Omar as the typically sensual man, fond of wine and the good

things of the world, suspicious of the professional expo-
nents of religion, and full of doubts about the purposes of
life here below and the reality of the hereafter. "The
quatrains here selected," says FitzGerald in the introduction to his poem, "are strung together into something of
an Eclogue, with perhaps a less than equal proportion
of the 'Drink and be merry' which (genuine or not) recurs
over-frequently in the Original." They show how "the
old Tentmaker, who, after vainly endeavouring to un-
shackle his Steps from Destiny, and to catch some glimpse
of Tomorrow, fell back upon To-day . . . as the only
Ground he got to stand upon, however momentarily
slipping from under his Feet."

FitzGerald's work is too familiar to need more than the
citation of a few quatrains to illustrate what was in general
his, rather than Omar's, philosophy of life. The first
voices his doubts about Tomorrow:

> Into this Universe, and *Why* not knowing
> Nor *Whence*, like Water willy-nilly flowing;
>   And out of it, as the Wind along the Waste,
> I know not *Whither*, willy-nilly blowing.[1]

The second by implication accuses Destiny of unfairness:

> Oh Thou, who didst with pitfall and with gin
> Beset the Road I was to wander in,
>   Thou wilt not with Predestined Evil round
> Enmesh and then impute my Fall to sin!

The following prose version of another quatrain presents
a different facet of the same picture, and reads:

> I am a miserable sinner; where is Thy grace?
> Where in my heart's recesses are Thy light and glory?
>   If Thou givest me Paradise for piety,
> 'Tis a bargain. Where lies Thy bounty then?

---

[1] The italics are FitzGerald's. Persian does not possess these indica-
tions of emphasis.

In rueful humor he calls out:

> Oh Wheel, your turning leaves me unrequited;
> Why give advice I cannot heed?
>   Your favour is all given to fools and wastrels.
> Well, I am not wise, nor am I deserving.

Conscious of his religious slackness he ironically attempts to placate the authorities by saying:

> Though I have never strung the pearls of piety,
> Ne'er wiped the smirch of sin from off my face,
>   I yet do not despair of Thy compassion,
> For never have I said that *One* was Two.

He left it to those authorities to decide whether he meant to express his conformity with the orthodox creed, "There is no God but Allah," or was speaking in the equivocal language of Sufism. As a professed Muslim and the child of his own day, Omar could not openly and without risk have admitted himself the author of sentiments which would have brought him into direct conflict with orthodoxy, whose teaching was that man's destiny hereafter was determined by his conduct here below, or alternatively that his destiny was fixed at the beginning of time. Quatrains of the nature just cited were derived from the common stock veiled in the anonymity in which Persians were accustomed to express their revolt against the unvarying forms of ritual, rigid doctrine, and dry-as-dust sermonizing. In the following verse the author, possibly Omar, speaks out boldly:

Hearts compounded by Him with the glory of Love,
Beat they in the Mosque or dwell in the Church,
    Let their owners' names be inscribed in the book of Love,
And they are free of Hell and careless of Heaven.

Put in another way:

Heathen temple and Muslim Kaʻba are houses of bondage;
The Ringing of bells is the music of bondage;
　　Girdle, church, prayer beads and cross—
All truly are tokens of bondage.

The following, attributed to Abu Saʻid ibn ʼl-Khair, expresses similar disregard for formal Muslim doctrine:

That burning fire entitled Love,
Clothed in heresy or in faith, is a raging fever.
　　The creed that calls on Allah and the religion of Love are
　　　　different things;
Yet the Prophet of Love is neither Arab nor Gentile.

Sometimes there is a protest from the human heart at all the mystic talk of allegorical love, and the poet has the courage to give vent to his feelings as a man. He says:

Love that's metaphor lacks all luster,
Like a half-dead fire its glow is dull.
　　He's true lover who day and night, year in year out,
Renouncing ease forgets both food and sleep.

Interwoven in the fabric of a great many quatrains like a somber thread is the brooding sense of man's helplessness in the clutch of a capricious yet all-powerful fate which makes his existence lack purpose, whatever the religion he professes. An illustration of such despondency is apparent in:

For Mosque I'm not suited nor fitted for Church;
God knows of what matter he kneaded my clay.
　　I'm poor as a pagan and drab as a whore,
Faithless and gearless, with Heaven remote.

It has been said by a European critic that not only the quatrains but all the songs of Persia are a hymn of revolt against the Koran, against the Pharisees, against the suppression of nature and common sense by the religious law. The man who drinks wine is for Khayyam the symbol of the emancipated human being; for the mystic wine is still more—it is the symbol of divine intoxication.

MATHNAVI

By contrast with the terseness of the ruba'i stands the expansiveness of the *mathnavi* form of verse. This is used for numerous long poems which, although less well known in the West than the lyrics or quatrains, are regarded by Persians as embodying some of the masterpieces of their literature. Some of these compositions run into thousands of lines and therefore demand a system of rhyming different from that of the shorter pieces, where the monorhyme was possible and usual. In the mathnavi each line consists of two hemistichs, or half-lines, rhyming together and independently of the other lines. It is similar to the "doublet" to be found in the narrative poems of the West, such as Chaucer's *Canterbury Tales* or the early French *Chanson de Geste*. That the form has a long history in Persia may be deduced from the numerous verse citations to be found in an old dictionary compiled by Asadi of Tus. A great many of these citations are in the mathnavi form and are taken from a metrical version made by Rudagi, the earliest celebrated poet of Iran, of the book of Buddhist fables known as *Kalila va Dimna*, or *The Fables of Bidpai*.

The form was used for epics, both narrative and romantic, and for didactic poems of all kinds, including ethics, history, religious doctrine, medicine, and even cookery. A very large number were devoted to the teachings of the Sufi mystics, one, the *Mathnavi-i Ma'navī* or *Spiritual Mathnavi* of Jalal al-Din Rumi, founder of the

Mevlevi order of dervishes, being numbered amongst the outstanding classics of Persian literature. As a rule, the meters used with the mathnavi form are different from those in use in the shorter poems such as ghazals and ruba'is.

In modern times in the West, didactic verse has been regarded as something aesthetically unworthy of consideration because it uses the language and forms of emotional art merely to expound matter-of-fact products of the intellect for which prose would be more suitable. The question is one largely of literary fashion. In Latin literature, Lucretius borrowed "the sweet voice of song" to expound the philosophical system of Epicurus, Virgil in the *Georgics* dealt with the cultivation of the land and gave exact precepts on how to plant the vine, and the *Ars Poetica* was intended by Horace to be useful as well as pleasing. In Persian there was hardly an art or science which was not at some period expounded in verse, but ethics, popular philosophy and, as has been said above, epic and romantic themes and Sufi lore supply the greatest mass of such "instructional" poetry.

43

THREE : PERSIAN PROSE

Our concern so far has been, as is traditional, with the beginnings and forms of poetry composed in the neo-Persian Islamic idiom. To Iranian taste, as has been seen, verse is preferable to prose, for the reason perhaps that the poet sings best in his mother tongue and so gets nearer to the heart of his audience. A contributory factor in the past may have been that the prose literature with which the Persians had been made familiar was in Arabic, associated in their minds with the sacred book and edifying discourses.

EARLY WORKS AND TRANSLATIONS

When the Arab conquerors had first overrun Persia, they entrusted to the *dihqans*, the peasant-proprietors mentioned earlier, the duty of revenue collection. These men learned the language of the new rulers and in course of time translated into Arabic the Pehlevi tax lists upon which they based their assessments. The extent of the country was vast, and, to assist government and other officials in their movements, route books were compiled, based probably upon original Pehlevi sources but after a time turned into Arabic. These compilations, having taxable land values as their prime objective, were full of geographical and economic details of immediate practical use to the government and of great historical interest to us as showing contemporary conditions in Iran. The men who did the work belonged to families with whom the profession was hereditary, particularly in Fars, which seems to have been the home of humanist and secular studies. Such men served the Coppersmith and other rulers in the preparation and description of "Routes and Districts," a title borne by more than one compilation. One of the earliest of the geographers whose works have survived was a certain Istakhri, who, as his name implies, was a native of Istakhr, the village which sprang up on the ruins of Persepolis, ancient capital of the Achaemenians. Another early geographer was Ibn Khurdadbih, a Magian who received Islam at the hands of the Barmecides. He became postmaster and intelligence officer to these Abbasid viziers in the mountain areas of Persian Iraq, but he was in addition a man of varied attainments who, as well as being the author of a book of routes and provinces, wrote on music, on the genealogies of the Persian kings, on cookery, games, and wine.

Of the same class as these travelers and surveyors were the scribes employed in a variety of capacities by the men who cut out provinces for themselves during the growth of Persian independence. Founders of new dynasties, great and small, were all anxious to demonstrate that they were of pure Iranian ancestry, amongst the most eager to do so being the men of humble origin. They got genealogists to construct elaborate family trees for them, and so it was that Ya'qub ibn Laith, the Coppersmith, could point with pride to his Sasanian ancestry, and the

45

sons of a humble villager, Buyah, or Buwaih, claim to be descended from the great warrior Bahram Gur, a famous Sasanian monarch. These Buyides by their prowess could well aspire to noble origins, for in the course of their martial career (945–1055) they overran the whole of western Persia and most of Iraq, where they held the caliph himself in their hands as an instrument of their own policy. But even a Turcoman slave such as Subuktagin, who founded the Ghaznavid empire on the ruins of that of the Samanids, displayed a pedigree that went back to Yazdigard, the Sasanian king of kings. The labors of the genealogists provided the materials for many books of annals, of which the Arabic-writing compilers made good use in their historical works.

In princely courts and cities alike the demand constantly grew for men of learning and skill in the professions that satisfied human requirements. A prince needed religious, legal, and political advisers, as well as officials who could carry out the administration of the government, which normally meant little more than the collecting of taxes. Prince and subjects alike required the services of physicians to cure their ailments, of stargazers to tell them how to order their affairs, of instructors in various arts to equip their minds, and of poets and storytellers to provide entertainment for their leisure hours.

On every facet of intellectual life thus represented, writings of comparatively early date have been preserved, all intended for princely courts. Very little has survived of the compositions addressed to humbler audiences—the crowd in the bazaar or the cultivators squatting round the ablution tank by the mosque in the village. In the early days education was, in Iran as elsewhere, a "mystery" confined to a select few. Amongst the Persians, the training which the nobility gave to their sons was in horsemanship and the arts of war. Very rarely did they concern themselves with reading and writing. As for the lesser folk, it was enough for them, or so said the nobles, to be apprenticed to trades in their youth. This, however, did not prevent their demanding and appreciating both verse and prose, and it may be assumed that they particularly relished the sallies of the parodists and satirists against the great, when the authorities, whether religious or political, were out of sight.

Even though education in letters was restricted to the few, there was a plentiful demand for books at princely courts and in cities. There is mention in quite early Muslim literature of copyists and booksellers who had shops in the bazaars. Some of them were authors in their own right and not unusually sold their own works as well as those of writers in general. As for libraries, the bibliographer Hajji Khalifa tells how the famous ninth-century anthology of ancient Arabic verse, the *Hamasa*, came into existence. Its compiler, Abu Tammam, has been on a visit from his home in Iraq to the court of the Tahirid prince Abd Allah in Khurasan, and on his way back found that the great highway over the Zagros range was blocked by snow. He accordingly turned back to the nearest town, which was Hamadan, where he was given hospitality in the house of a Persian grandee. There he found a rich library and settled down happily for the winter, occupying his time by extracting from manuscripts the passages which went to make up one of the classics of Arabic literature. And a library of this kind cannot have been unique, because many a prince and vizier is mentioned by the biographers as having possessed a notable collection of books.

For at least the first three centuries after the Arab occupation, many such books must still have been written in Pehlevi, as we learn from incidental references in a variety of sources. Tabari, in his huge "Annals of the

47

Apostles and Kings," in reporting the famous trial of the Iranian warrior Afshin in the year 225 of the Hegira (840) tells how the accused man, who was a fairly recent convert of Islam, was asked by the prosecutor, "What is that book in your possession that you have had ornamented with gold, jewels, and brocade, and is full of heresies?" He answered, "I inherited it from my father. It contains Persian literature, and, as for what you call heresies, I have contented myself with the literary portion and left everything else aside. I found it as it is, with its ornamentation, and, seeing no need to remove the jewels, I left them. In the same way you possess the book of *Kalila va Dimna* and the Book of Mazdak in your own house. I did not think that that excluded me from Islam."

From the Arabic-writing historian Mas'udi we learn further that in the year 303 of the Hegira (915–916) he had seen at Istakhr, on the site of the ancient Persepolis, a book which had been found in the treasury of the Iranian kings and was translated into Arabic for the benefit of the Umayyad caliph Hisham (724–743). It contained accounts of the ancient sciences, annals, architecture, and governmental institutions, as well as portraits of the Sasanian kings and queens. In another part of his work Mas'udi describes a great book that he had found in the year 345 of the Hegira (956) in the house of a priest high up in the Zoroastrian hierarchy. It was a portion of a "Book of Laws" that enumerated the great variety of classes into which the common people of Iran, as distinct from the nobility, were divided.

As happened with poetry, Persian secular prose blossomed against the background of Arabic and Pehlevi writings. The earliest surviving examples were in fact translations from Arabic, but apart from occasional archaisms, they are as normal specimens of Persian writing as were produced later directly in Persian. They may

have passed through the hands of redactors who modern-
ized a word here and there in the course of the years,
but the style is polished, speaking of long precedent and
training. By the time that writers were being attracted
to the Samanid courts, the literary language was firmly
established. It is not easy to judge of this from translations, but a couple of specimens may provide some idea
of the directness with which a narrative is set out, un-
hampered by accumulations of synonyms, involved
syntax, and far-fetched metaphors which were too often
apparent in later prose.

The first is from the introduction to a prose "Book of
Kings" that was one of the sources from which Firdausi
drew materials for his classic *Shahnama*. This book was
the work of one Abu Mansur al-Mu'ammari, who completed it in 957, having been induced to undertake the
task by his master, Abu Mansur, son of Abd al-Razzaq.

The amir Abu Mansur was a person of fine presence and strong
will, having a good mind and a generous nature, and by the
power of absolute rulership he kept harmony amongst the
nobles. His ideals were lofty, and he could trace his ancestry
back to a family of noble stock, originating in the seed of warrior
chieftains of Iran. The story [of the importation from India]
of the book of *Kalila va Dimna* was once brought to his ears and
interested him so much that he prayed fortune to grant him a
similar memorial in this world. Accordingly he bade his vizier
Abu Mansur al-Mu'ammari to assemble the owners of books—
whether *dihqans*, men of learning, or men of experience of the
world—from the various cities. I, therefore, his servant, Abu
Mansur al-Mu'ammari, at his command had a message prepared and taken to the cities of Khurasan by one who brought
from there men of alert mind, such as Saiyah, son of the
Khurasani Azhari; Yazdan-dad from Sistan; Mahuvi Khur-
shid from Nishapur; and Shadan from Tus. Having gathered
these four together, he set them to the task of collating the
annals of the kings and the records of their achievements,

49

writing the biography of each, with his fate (just or unjust), the rebellions with which he dealt, his wars, and his legislation. They were to begin with the first king who ever lived in the world and introduced human conduct, distinguishing mankind from other animals, and go down to Yazdigard, the last of the Iranian kings.

The historians completed their task in the month of Muharram of the year 346 of the Hegira [957] of the Best in the Universe, Muhammad the Chosen (Allah bless him and secure him well-being!), and they called the work "The Book of the Kings." In it men of understanding may read and learn the wisdom of kings, nobles, and sages (that is, the achievements and designs of kingship), their disposition and conduct, their beneficial institutions, equity and administration of justice, their ways of transacting affairs and their military administration, their methods of waging war, conquering cities, exacting vengeance, launching attacks, winning victory, and imposing conditions.

BAL'AMI'S ANNALS

Another work in the early Persian literary style is that usually known as "Bal'ami's Annals," composed, or rather adapted from an Arabic original, by a vizier, Bal'ami, belonging to a long line of court officials who in their time were second only in importance to the Barmecides who served the Abbasid caliphs. This Bal'ami was minister of the Samanid Mansur ibn Nuh, who ruled Transoxiana and Khurasan from 961 to 976, and he continued the annals until the year of the Hegira 355 (966), the original ones, compiled by the famous Arabic-writing historian Tabari, having ceased with the Hegira year 302. Again we have simple narrative, as in the following anecdote "The Wild Ass," related about Bahram Gur, known to English readers from one of FitzGerald's quatrains:

One day Bahram, with an escort of Arabs, and Munzir (King of Hira, at whose court he had been brought up) went out hunting and saw in the distance a wild ass running across the plain. With Munzir and the escort following, he set out in pursuit, fitted an arrow into his bowstring, and loosed it. When he came up with the ass, he found that a lion had leapt upon it, and, with its teeth buried in the ass's neck was on the point of slaying it. He shot another arrow, which hit the lion in the back, passed through its belly into the ass's back, and, having penetrated that, plunged up to half its length firmly into the ground. For a while ass and lion writhed together, then both fell dead. The bystanders were filled with amazement, and he [Munzir] ordered that a picture of the ass, the lion, and the whole scene should be painted on the walls of Bahram's palace in the capital.

That picture, or rather a miniature of it, is to be found in a great many manuscripts of the *Shahnama*, and of the romantic epics based on it.

Regularly amongst the men of learning and accomplishment who gathered about royal courts there were some to ensure the physical welfare of the prince and his family; others whose business was to advise on political, religious, and ethical questions; and still others who provided edification and amusement. From very early times "wisdom" literature has formed an important part of the writings of the East, figuring prominently in such scriptural books as Ecclesiastes, Job, and Proverbs, and frequently also in Sanskrit literature. It was not lacking in neo-Persian literature, various books of wise saws having from time to time been compiled for the guidance of princes and rulers. Two of the best known were produced in the second half of the eleventh century, in the period of the Seljuq Turcoman rulers, who, originating in Central Asia, had swept away the native dynasties reigning in Persia, Iraq, Syria, and Asia Minor and established their own widespread empire there.

KAI KA'US: THE ANDARZ-NAMA

One of the works in question was that variously known as *Andarz-nama* (*Book of Counsel*) or *Qabus-nama* (*Book of Qabus*), composed for the benefit of his son by Kai Ka'us ibn Iskandar ibn Qabus. He was a member of the once powerful dynasty of the Ziyarids, who had reigned in the provinces bordering the southern shores of the Caspian Sea until they were reduced to vassalship of the Seljuqs. None of the family bore a very enviable reputation, but Kai Ka'us was loyal to his favorite son and in this work endeavored to provide him with the fruits of his own personal experience, outlining a number of possible courses to meet likely or unlikely eventualities. In general he showed him how to enjoy life as it comes and how to stand against the winds of change and the caprices of fortune.

Here and there an artless little piece of verse is put in to add emphasis to a point, or possibly to give light relief from the monotony of prose. In the course of his precepts and admonishings the author imagines the contingencies that might arise in the uncertain political conditions of the time, when a man might be thrown on his own resources and have to adopt very unfamiliar shifts in order to keep alive. There are instructions on what to do and how to behave if one had to become a wandering dervish or a merchant in the bazaar, a physician or a judge, a vizier or—for even that possibility is not ruled out—a king. A whole chapter, for example, is devoted to minstrelsy, concerning which profession the author says:

My son, if you become a musician, you need to be of cheerful spirit and sharp wit. Keep yourself always cleanly dressed, fragrant and perfumed. And let your tongue be smooth; if you come to a house for minstrelry, do not enter with a sour face and a reserved expression. Do not play measures that are all serious, nor yet all that are lively. It would be out of place to confine yourself to a single mode; all men are not of the same nature and, consequently, if they vary in constitution they also vary in disposition. For that reason the master musicians devised a system for this art. They first composed a "royal" melody, to be played in company where kings were present, and then set down pieces in a solemn measure to which songs can be sung. That is the kind of music suited to elderly men and close to the mood of serious people. They realized, however, that not everyone is old or serious and so decided after making provision for them to provide also for the young. They cast about for lyrics in a more spirited mood and set them to lively tunes, so that the minstrel could then play both to old and young. But also, in order that women and children and even persons very given to levity should not be left neglected, they composed melodies for their benefit.

NIZAM AL-MULK: THE SIYASAT-NAMA

The second of the two works referred to is the *Siyasat-nama*, composed by the famous vizier Nizam al-Mulk for the benefit of his sovereign the Seljuq sultan Malikshah. Its subject matter is on a less personal plane than that of the *Qabus-nama*, though touching it at numerous points as being intended to provide guidance for the prince in the government of the realm, its organization, its offices, and its general welfare. An important supplement is concerned with the dangers to which the state is liable through the employment of heretics, by which are meant the followers of religions or beliefs not held by the ruler or his advisers and whose loyalties therefore might be suspect. Since nonconformity in matters of religion almost always implied political discontent and unrest, it was of importance to the state that heresies be suppressed. Nizam al-Mulk had a particular reason for personal concern in this matter, for he felt that certain highly placed officers of the state belonged to one of the factions of the Shi'a known as Batinis or Ismailis, who afterward became notorious as the "Assassins" and at whose hands he met his death before his book was actually completed or its advice could be put into practice by the sultan. Something of the character of the "wisdom" imparted by Nizam al-Mulk may be gathered from the chapter on military organization, which reads:

If an army is composed entirely of men of the same origins, there is a risk involved because they do not exert themselves properly and may become turbulent. The force should be made up from different [regional] groups, two thousand from the Dailam [Caspian] and Khurasan provinces being stationed in the capital. Those already there should be kept and any others reorganized, although if they are Georgians or men of Shaban-kara in Fars that would be permissible, because they are men of good quality. It used to be the practice of Sultan Mahmud [of Ghazna] to constitute his army of men from different regions, namely Turks, Khurasanis, Arabs, Indians, Dailamites, and Ghuris. When there was an expedition afoot, notice was given each night about the contingent from each group required to compose the guard, each having its station allotted, from which none dared to move until dawn because of risks from the others. If there was fighting during the day, each group had its own battle order and fought its utmost for the glory of its name and repute, with the result that no one ever complained of a group's having shown cowardice in the battle. When the organization of warriors is carried out in that way, they will all show keenness to fight and be eager to make a name for themselves, so that when they put their hands to their weapons they will never withdraw before they have broken their opponents. Having once or twice got the upper hand and beaten their foes, a hundred of their cavalry will treat with disregard a thousand of the enemy, for no one will be able to stand against troops as victorious as these. The forces of neighboring lands would be overcome with fear of any king having troops of this kind, and would make their submission to him.

Iran had been under Muslim domination for nearly six centuries when it was struck by a wave of calamity from Central Asia, where the Mongol hordes had burst their bounds and overflowed into Transoxiana and Persia. This was the most devastating of a long series of destructive invasions that had descended from Central Asia, the earlier ones having come from the Ghuzz Turks. The Mongols were not indiscriminate in their choice of victims, but any obstacle such as a walled city was razed to the ground and its institutions wiped out. It was not that the Mongol leaders were closely attached to any faith. They were in fact indifferent to what their subjects believed, but they wiped out religious or political institutions or personalities that might become a focus of resistance to their own overriding will, doing irreparable harm in the process to the civilized life of the Iranians. Yet the Mongol chieftains were not without their own conception of the qualities an educated man should possess and of the value of certain sides of intellectual life. It was during their rule over Iran that the best histories produced in Persian were written, two in particular outstanding for the excellence of their prose style. These were the work of Persians who were high up in the service of the Mongol state but contrived to reconcile their inward convictions with loyalty to their masters, at whose hands, nevertheless, they subsequently met torment and death.

JUVAINI: HISTORY OF THE WORLD-CONQUEROR

The earlier of the two authors indicated was 'Ala al-Din (Aladdin), 'Ata Malik Juvaini, a native of the district of Juvain in Khurasan and son of a minister in the Mongol service. His *History of the World-Conqueror* deals with the Mongols from 1206, when Chingiz Khan amalgamated

55

a number of Central Asian tribes under his sole leadership, down to 1256, when his nephew Hulagu led an expedition against the Ismaili Assassins and destroyed their chief stronghold at Alamut in northwest Persia. Juvaini accompanied the Mongol commander of this expedition and was given the task of drawing up the terms of surrender and presenting them to the last Grand Master of the Assassins. When the castle had been thrown open to the victors, Juvaini examined the contents of the treasury and picked out a number of instruments used in astronomy or astrology that he thought might be acceptable to his master. Similarly he went through the numerous volumes which had been accumulating in the library there for a great many years, laying aside those that he considered rare or valuable and destroying anything heretical. Amongst those he saved was the book containing the "adventures" of Hasan-i Sabbah, the first Grand Master of the Order of the Assassins, with the Syrian branch of whose family the Crusaders came into such dramatic contact. Both Juvaini and Rashid al-Din, the second of the historians above mentioned, incorporated parts of these memoirs in their own books. When Hulagu resumed operations after the surrender of the Assassins, he marched on Baghdad, which soon succumbed to him, and there he appointed Juvaini to the governorship, granting him a free hand in the control of affairs.

Some idea of the colorful style of the *History of the World-Conqueror*, with its wealth of imagery and metaphor —and, incidentally, of the Mongols' campaigning methods —may be gathered from the extract describing how the advance on Bukhara was made:

Once Chingiz Khan had completed the reorganization and equipment of his armies, he advanced upon the territories of the sultan [of Khwarazm]. He sent his elder sons and chieftains by alternative routes, each in command of a strong force, while he in person set out with the object of attacking Bukhara itself. His lieutenant was Tuli, one of his elder sons, and his army was composed of Turks, undauntable warriors who made no distinction of clean and unclean, looked on war drums as bowls of smooth liquor, and saw their daily portion in morsels cut out by the sword. Their route lay by Zarnuq. One morning, when the king of planets raised his banner above the horizon of the east, they suddenly arrived on the outskirts of the town, whose inhabitants had no inkling of the vicissitudes that had come about in the course of the days and the nights.

As they gazed about them they saw the ground on every side covered with mounted men and the air black as night with the dust raised by the horses. Terror, nay panic, took possession of them and a fearsome dread gained control. They seized the citadel [i.e., the city's strong point] and locked the gates. Then, thinking that it was perhaps only one troop of a large army, or a solitary wave from an overflowing tide, they proposed to offer resistance, thus advancing to destruction on their own feet. It was only by the aid of the Lord's mercy that they halted their steps and breathed no word of opposition.

In the interval, the Lord of the World [i.e., Chingiz], as was his practice, sent his chamberlain Danishmand with a message proclaiming the arrival of his legions and warning the inhabitants to refrain from crossing that awe-inspiring torrent. Some of them, obeying the decree contained in the phrase "Satan possessed them," were on the point of offering him violence and inflicting injury on him when he called out, "I am Thus-and-Thus, a Muslim and son of a Muslim. In accordance with the will of God and the mighty decree of Chingiz Khan, I have come with a message that will deliver you from the maelstrom of destruction and the vat of shed blood. It is Chingiz Khan who is here in person, with many thousands of warriors. Should he find any trace of resistance to him, in an instant your citadel will be leveled with the ground and the whole plain turned to a sea of blood. But if you will listen attentively, with the ear of common sense, to advice and good counsel and submit yourselves obediently to his commands, your lives and possessions will remain in the fortress of security."

57

When the inhabitants, high and low, heard his words, which bore the mark of honesty, they paid heed and without hesitation accepted his advice, recognizing that a torrent cannot be stemmed by blocking the channel nor the quaking of mountains and plains be made to subside or be calmed by the pressure of feet. They realized it was to their interest to behave peaceably and to their advantage to accept the advice given. But out of caution and for their peace of mind they demanded a bond from him to the effect that he would be responsible if, once the inhabitants had come out to receive him and had acknowledged his authority, any single one of them should suffer harm. After that they took comfort, suppressed any idea directed towards wrongdoing and set their hands to honorable dealing.

The elders and principal inhabitants of Zarnuq then delegated a number of themselves to go forward with gifts. On reaching the encampment of the king's [i.e., Chingiz's] army, he inquired who were the chief citizens and notables of Zarnuq and showed his displeasure that [so many] had remained in retirement in the background. He sent a messenger to bring them into his presence, at which [show of] royal authority a shuddering fell upon the limbs of the whole company like the quaking upon the sides of a mountain. They immediately set out to present themselves before his Majesty, who, on their arrival, treated them with clemency and graciousness and granted them security for their lives, so that they recovered confidence. He then commanded that every dweller in the city, whosoever it might be, alike the wearers of the religious doctor's cap and turban and the [woman's] wimple and veil, should come out. The citadel was razed to the ground. After counting heads, boys and young men were assigned to forced labor at Bukhara, while the rest were permitted to return home.

RASHID AL-DIN: COMPENDIUM OF HISTORIES

The second of the two notable histories produced in the Mongol period was the work of Rashid al-Din Fadl

58

Allah, "Rashid the Physician," as he sometimes called himself. He had begun his service with the Mongols as physician to Abaqa, the son of Hulagu, but later became chief minister to Abaqa's grandsons Ghazan (1295–1305) and Uljaitu (1304–1316), members of the independent Il-Khan dynasty of Persia. In that position he enjoyed wide powers, which he wielded for nearly twenty years. His *Compendium of Histories* was based partly on his personal knowledge and partly on what he learned from the well-instructed envoys from many nations who came to the Mongol court, "each of whom is a volume of the annals, legends, and beliefs of his own people." Originally it was intended to be a history of Chingiz Khan and his ancestors and successors, but in its final form it also included a great deal of general history, gathered from conversations with the court visitors, some of whom translated passages of their own books for his benefit. Thus we find in his book the story of the world as related by Iranian legend, from Kayumarth, the first human king, to the prophet Muhammad, then accounts of the ancient Turks, the Chinese, the Israelites, the Franks, and the Indians, as well as scriptural history according to the Christians, a geography of the lands of Christendom and their kings, and biographies of the popes and emperors. This miscellany contains some material not available elsewhere, but its main value lies on the literary side, as an excellent piece of writing free of the faults that later vitiated the rhetorical type of Persian prose.

These two histories were produced at a time when the Mongol rulers of Persia had broken away from the great khans in China and founded their own dynasty of the Il-Khans. Ghazan and his successors in fact adopted Islam, and in course of time the Mongols were absorbed into the general body of Iranians much as the Arabs had been. Their merit in their early days was that they

59

provided the country with a unity it had lacked for centuries, even though it was a unity of desolation, and they forced a centralized government upon the people. Being at a very primitive stage of organization, they knew little or nothing of the art of government, but they supplied the military backing for the Persians they employed in their administration. In the end, their heavy demands of manpower for military and labor services and constant pressure for money and materials reduced people and land to a state of poverty and disorder leading finally to ruin. Scholars and men of letters had little place in their scheme of things. Numbers emigrated, so that some of the outstanding personages in the world of contemporary Persian literature produced their work abroad, well-known figures among them being the most famous of all Sufi poets, Maulavi Jalal al-Din, commonly entitled "Rumi" (The Man of Rum, i.e., Asia Minor), author of the *Mathnavi-i Ma'navi* (*Spiritual Mathnavi*).

SA'DI OF SHIRAZ

The southern region of Persia suffered rather less from the Mongol depredations than the northern, largely because the local rulers, such as the Atabegs, who succeeded the Seljuqs in Fars, and the Qara Khita'i in Kirman, hastened to declare their submission at the first threat of the onslaught. Yet here too the menacing shadow of the Mongol approach had its effect. Members of the educated class fled before it, amongst them being Sa'di, whose name stands high on the scroll of fame in Persia, where he is commonly referred to as "the Sheik." Details about his life which have not been in dispute are rare, but it is almost certain that he was born in Shiraz, the capital of Fars, at a date not verifiable, fled to Baghdad before the Mongol advance, and there studied at the important

Nizamiya college founded by the famous Seljuq vizier Nizam al-Mulk. Upon leaving the college, he started out on a roving life as a dervish, wandering in his travels through Mesopotamia, Asia Minor, Syria, and Egypt, and making more than one pilgrimage to Mecca. There is a hint in one of his books of his having fallen into the hands of the Crusaders in Syria and having served them as a galley slave, but that may be artistic invention.

Sa'di returned to his native Shiraz in 1256, or a year later, and there settled down to a life of authorship in which he was able to utilize his many colorful experiences, and his imagination, to great effect. The result was a literary output which brought him enormous fame while he was still alive. Although a study of his poetry must be postponed until we reach a consideration of the ghazal writers, two of his works may appropriately be mentioned at once: one, the *Bustan* (*The Scented Garden*), entirely in mathnavi verse, and the other, the *Gulistan* (*The Rose Garden*), in a mixture of prose and verse. To this day they are constantly being quoted by Persians to heighten the force of an argument or to lend additional color to a story, much as *Hamlet* or other Shakespearean works are in English. Both Sa'di's compositions preach the standard virtues of humility, charity, and tolerance, but they also reflect the social conditions of their age by combining lofty ideals with a practical and worldly philosophy based upon common sense. This comes out well in the first story in the *Gulistan*, where the moral is that a lie which makes for peace and goodwill is preferable to a truth that stirs up strife, and the doctrine of enlightened self-interest finds support in the story of the wrestling champion who, in a decisive match, beats a dangerous opponent who had once been his own pupil.

There once lived a man who had reached the summit of his profession as a wrestler. He knew three hundred and sixty different holds, of which he exhibited a fresh one each day. To one of his pupils, a handsome youth for whom he had great affection, he taught three hundred and fifty-nine, but one special hold he kept to himself. The youth advanced in skill and strength to such a pitch that no one was a match for him, and he one day boasted in the sultan's presence that he only conceded superiority to the champion out of respect for his years and gratitude for his tutelage, he himself being in strength not inferior and in skill equal. The sovereign frowned on this presumption and commanded that a match be held.

A wide open space was prepared for the occasion, and the ministers of the state and grandees of the court all attended. Like an elephant in rage the youth attacked with a charge that would have moved a mountain of iron from its base, but the master met it with the hold that he had kept to himself and which the youth had not the skill to counter. The champion lifted him from the ground, raised him over his head, and dashed him to the ground, at which the crowd roared. On the champion the king bestowed a robe of honor and a purse of money, and to the pupil he expressed his disapprobation and contempt for his arrogance in challenging his benefactor—and failing. The young man remarked, "He won by a wrestling trick which he did not teach me," whereupon the older man said, "It was on purpose for such an occasion as this that I reserved it, for the sages say, 'Never put yourself so completely in the hands of a friend that he will have you in his power should he ever become your enemy.'"

From the early Samanid times onwards an abundance of works in the neo-Persian prose is recorded by the bibliographers under a great variety of headings—history, science, arts and crafts, theology, philosophy, medicine, mathematics, and the like—all of them interesting to the specialist rather than to the general reader. In addition there is an immense quantity of technical Sufi literature, supplemented by many volumes of biographies of Sufi saints and poets. Romantic fiction occupies a good deal of space in the lists. Some are tales of heroic adventure running to many thousands of words, others collections of anecdotes or fables grouped round some central theme. One example of the latter is known as "Relief after Stress" and consists of stories of people who have by a miracle or sudden chance escaped death, or have found joy after suffering the pangs of love. Another kind of collective volume resembles the *Arabian Nights* in being a series of tales introduced by a "master" tale or else fitted into a framework.

FOUR : FIRDAUSI AND
NIZAMI

The writers whom the Persians hold to be masters in the literary field are, apart from Sa'di, not historians or other compilers of prose works but their poets. These are their pride, the names most often on their lips being Firdausi of Tus (approximately the modern Mashhad), Sheik Sa'di of Shiraz, Maulavi Jalal al-Din of Rum, and Khwaja Hafiz of Shiraz, with a few others, like Nizami of Ganja and Mulla Jami of the town of Jam (in Khurasan), a little less often.

First in time and perhaps second only to Sa'di in general esteem comes Firdausi, whose genius and un-remitting labors produced the *Shahnama* and brought it to fame. He himself tells us that the work had been begun by Daqiqi of Tus, a young man of talent who became a panegyrist of the Samanids. In 980 Daqiqi was murdered by his Turkish slave, for reasons that can only be surmised, leaving the poem in a rudimentary form. It then consisted of about a thousand verses—dealing with the rise of Zoroaster and the establishment of his religion—which Firdausi incorporated in what he regarded as an appropriate place in the poem, together with some unflattering comments on their quality. Why, under the circumstances, he retained them at all is a matter for speculation, one conjecture being that they provided evidence of his orthodoxy, which was at one time attacked on the score of his showing favor to Zoroastrianism, the ancient faith of Iran, or else of his being an adherent of the Shi'a heresy.

However that may be, the verses proved finally to be only a very small part of the whole *Shahnama*, which Firdausi continued from a prose version and which ultimately reached a length of about forty thousand *baits*, or lines. It is indeed a work on the heroic scale, beginning with an account of the creation of the universe, advancing majestically through the mythical and legendary ages of the heroes, and finishing on a note of realism with the fall of Yazdigard, the last king of the Sasanian dynasty. The style is generally regarded by Europeans as undistinguished, largely because adherence to the same meter throughout a long work induces a feeling of monotony, not entirely relieved even by the way in which the rhyme is changed from one line to the next. The basis of the meter (the *mutaqarib*) is a foot of three syllables, one short followed by two long (⌣ — —), four times repeated in each half-line, but with the last foot, that which bears the rhyme, abbreviated to a short syllable followed by one long one.[1]

So far as the nature of the contents is concerned, the *Shahnama*, although intended for recital at royal courts,

[1] A short syllable consists of a consonant bearing a short vowel, while a long one is a combination of a consonant with a long vowel or two consonants with an intervening vowel, the second consonant remaining unvoweled. If a syllable ends in two unvoweled consonants, such a long syllable may be followed for metrical purposes by a short syllable supplied in scansion if not represented in the text.

is as near an approach to popular storytelling as has ever "come off the road" into Persian literature. It recalls the improviser in the marketplace with his stock of heroic tales, both dramatic and romantic; lyrics; and fairy tales all mixed up together. In early times the saga or epic transmitted what was looked upon as history, and in Firdausi's day this was still true. But it had by then become the driving force and mainstay of national sentiment and patriotism. The *Shahnama* is indeed an epic of the people such as no other nation has ever produced, with its materials going back to the beginning of time, some being familiar to a Greek author like Ctesias, a doctor at the Persian court about 400 B.C. who wrote a history of Persia. Firdausi therefore did not invent the legends he set down, but transmitted in verse form a general picture of the past glories of Iran, which from its appearance on the stage of history played an important part in civilizing the world.

The whole story is presented in gigantic outlines surpassing Wagner's *Valhalla*, and the events and characters described suffer no terrestrial limits as they range widely over earth and sky. In general the heroes live and wage war for hundreds of years, kings from the height of their thrones dictate their commands to the whole world and proclaim themselves the direct instruments of God's will. There is a theatrical and fairy-tale atmosphere about it all; every scene and every character is bathed in the sharp brilliance of a Persian summer sunrise. The king's treasuries and stores are inexhaustibly full of money and materials, and if any royal personage has need of something it appears instantaneously. Armies hundreds of thousands strong are mobilized overnight, no question ever arising about transport or supply. The great champions have the stature and strength of Titans and live many times the span of human existence, so that when the death of any one of them is announced in the narrative it comes with the force of a shock. Yet here and there a graphic detail is put in which can reduce a scene or a personality to human dimensions.

The theme that runs throughout the whole poem is, as has been indicated, the rise and career of the Iranian people, and especially their struggle against Turan. This is linked with the conflict between good and evil, where good must in the long run prevail, and also with the constant insistence upon the text that loyalty to his sovereign must be every man's first concern. The story, after an introduction by the author, begins with the creation of the world "out of nothingness." Then the primeval kings are shown in rather unsophisticated fashion introducing the basic implements of civilization into the world, the narrative taking on a more colorful and less prosaic aspect when it comes to deal with the reign of Jamshid, who was king for seven hundred years. We are told how in the course of his rule the evil and tyrannical monster Zahhak, out of whose shoulders grew serpents which demanded the brains of youths and maidens for their nutriment each day, was overthrown by the combined efforts of Kaveh the Blacksmith and the royal prince Faridun. When his children fell victims to the evil appetite of Zahhak, Kaveh fought heroically against the monster and achieved such fame that his leathern apron became the Iranian palladium.

When Faridun in due course became king, he divided the world between his three sons, one of whom, Iraj, was slain out of jealousy by the other two, Salm and Tur. Thus began the blood feud which existed ever after between Iran and Turan. Vengeance for his father's death was exacted by Minuchihr, son of Iraj, and it is while he rules over Iran that the heroic Sam appears. He is father of Zal, an albino who falls in love with

Rudaba, daughter of Mihrab, king of Kabul, descended from the monstrous Zahhak. Of their union is born Rustam, the great hero of the Iranian saga. Rustam's battles for his fatherland are numberless and his famous steed Rakhsh often figures in them, so that in the miniatures which frequently adorn the pages of the *Shahnama* the man is rarely shown without the horse.

One of Rustam's exploits is the tragic encounter in which he killed his son Suhrab, a theme used to great effect in a poem by Matthew Arnold. It is the pathos of the story which caught the fancy of both Firdausi and the English poet, for the actual battle scene is not one of the best depicted in the *Shahnama*. More telling is the account of the campaign which Rustam waged, in alliance with the braggart king Ka'us, against Mazandaran, the land of the Demons. Rustam first delivers to the king of Mazandaran a message from Ka'us demanding his surrender; when that demand is rejected, he returns home to prepare with his ally for the forthcoming war, the foeman becoming similarly engaged.

When Rustam turned away from Mazandaran,
   the wizard king [thereof] prepared for war.
He caused a pavilion to be hauled outside the city
   and led his troops out on the plain,
So numerous that when their dust rose up
   the color of the sun was hidden,
The plain could not be seen, nor vale nor mountain,
   and the earth was trampled flat by tramp of elephants.
This force he drove ahead swiftly as the wind,
   seeking never a moment to slacken his pace.
When news arrived to Ka'us the king
   that the army of the Demons was approaching,
He ordered that Rustam son of Zalzar
   should foremost gird up his loins for the fray.
To Tus and to Gudarz and the sons of Kashwad,
   to Giw and to Gurgin, those mighty nobles,

68

He gave command to make their forces ready,
   equipping them with spears and shields.
The pavilion for the king and for the chieftains
   they transported to the plain of Mazandaran.
On the right flank stationed himself Tus the son of Nauzar—
   the heart of the mountain echoed with the trumpet blast;
Upon the left were men like Gudarz and Kashwad—
   it was as though the mass were a mountain of iron;
In the center was the commander, Ka'us;
   all about him the warriors drawn up in array.
Before the troops stood he of the elephant body [Rustam],
   who never in battle had witnessed defeat.
From the Mazandaran [army] came forth a man of fame,
   upon his shoulder a massive battle-ax.
Juya [Seeker] was his name, and in truth he was a seeker of
      repute,
   a wielder of the ax and of a ready tongue.
By license of the king Juya stepped forward
   and hastened towards the commander Ka'us.
The armor shone upon his body,
   the flame of his sword set the earth alight.
Advancing thus he passed before the Iranians,
   mountain and vale reechoing to his tread.
Said he, "Who seeks to do me battle?
   What man is he that can raise dust from water?"
To do battle with Juya no man stepped forward,
   you might have said no nerve was stirred, no blood moved
      in a vein.
Then spake the king aloud,
   "What ails you, valiant and doughty men,
That at this Demon your heart so quails,
   that at his challenge all your faces darken?"
To the king the warriors gave no answer,
   as though by Juya the army was laid waste.
'Twas then that Rustam touched his horse's rein;
   laying his shining spear along its neck
He said, "Let but the king his license grant me
   to stand against this evildoing Demon."

69

Thus spoke King Ka'us, "This task is yours indeed.
   No other in Iran would seek this battle.
Go, and may the Creator be your aid!
   May every Demon and wizard be your prey!"
He spurred the gallant Rakhsh [his horse] ahead,
   in his grasp a skull-crushing spear,
And to the battleground charged like an elephant in rage,
   under him a leopard, a dragon in his hand.
As he turned the reins the dust flew up,
   the battleground shuddering with the sound of it.
To Juya he cried out, "Ill-omened creature,
   whose name's rejected by all free men.
You stand now in a sorry plight,
   this is no time for confidence and ease.
Let her that bore you now shed tears for you;
   let her bite her hand with growing anguish."
Juya answered, "Be not so carefree
   with Juya and his head-harvesting sword.
Let your mother's heart now break for you,
   let her weep over this armor and helmet of yours."
Rustam heard these words out to the end,
   then raised his voice and spoke his name.
From his place he strode like a mountain moving
   while his rival's soul was steeped in gloom.
He twisted his rein and turned away his face
   lacking desire to do battle with Rustam.
From that famed warrior he fled in panic;
   But Rustam uttered a lion's roar,
Pursued him close as his very dust,
   couched a spear in the girdle at his waist
And struck where backplate joined into armor,
   leaving in the armor no loop or knot unbroken.
From the saddle he parted him and raised him aloft,
   like a fowl on a spit he twirled him about,
Off his horse's back thrust him down in the dust,
   his mouth full of dirt and his armor in pieces.

After a stern and extended battle Ka'us and Rustam
succeeded in overthrowing the Demons of Mazandaran

and, using them as slaves, forced them into the labor of building two splendid palaces in the Elburz mountains. From the description Firdausi gives, it is clear that the region was a favorite part of Iran with him. If there is anything approaching "pastoral" poetry in Persian literature, it is to be found here, where a picture is provided of the setting for a Golden Age: "Elysian regions where we are to meet with nothing but joy and plenty and contentment, where every gale whispers pleasure and every shade promises repose."[1] According to Firdausi, it was:

Such a spot as the heart delighted in,
    where day lingered long and never diminished.
No blazing July was ever seen here, nor icy December;
    its air was all perfume, its rain fell as wine.
All the year round its climate breathed springtime
    and its blossoms were lovely as rosy-cheeked maids.
Hearts remained far removed from pain, grief, and care;
    a Demon's body was there to suffer all ill.
Day's head there sunk down in slumber,
    having taught a lesson of goodness and right.

After numerous diversions, often more interesting than the main theme itself, of which the thread sometimes disappears, the story reaches the reign of Gushtasp, when Zoroaster comes to establish his new religion. Isfandiyar, the king's son, turns into a strong supporter of the faith, and it is he who leads the army of Iran when war with Turan flares up anew. He brings the war to an end, but is slain in combat with Rustam, who himself soon afterward meets his doom. We then come to the Alexander story, in a mixture of history and legend, and lastly to the Sasanian period, for whose social and political conditions the *Shahnama* might serve as a textbook, so many are the details which it incidentally supplies.

[1] Dr. Samuel Johnson in 1750.

It is a man's world that is depicted. Woman is a creature designed for his pleasure and for procreation, or else she is an Amazon, who takes such virile part in battles as to overthrow established warriors. Firdausi has the traditional Persian view of what constitutes the ideal wife:

Three virtues a woman must possess to adorn a royal throne,
First, she must have modesty and also wealth, with which
   her consort may adorn his house.
Then she must bear a noble son,
   to increase her husband's happiness.
Third, she must be handsome both of figure and of face,
   and, though veiled, her spirit must shine through.

As for what constitutes feminine beauty, there is the charming little sketch of Rudaba, who won the heart of Zal:

Within his [her father's] veiled apartment there's a maid
   whose face is brighter than the sun;
From head to foot she's [white] as ivory,
   her cheek like Heaven, her form a willow's;
Upon her silvern shoulders lie two tresses dark,
   their ends like the rings of fetters;
Her mouth a pomegranate blossom, her lip a cherry,
   from her silvern breasts grow two pomegranate seeds,
Her eyes are two narcissi in the garden;
   her lashes stolen from a raven's wing.

In general woman is a weak vessel, whose counsel is never to the point and taken by man only at his peril. Isfandiyar, son of the Iranian king Gushtasp, having on a certain occasion received his mother's advice, replies:

To woman never tell your inward secret, for if you do
   you'll find it lying in the street;
Never perform a woman's behest,
   for you'll never see a woman whose counsel is sound.

Yet instances of chivalry towards women are recorded on fairly numerous occasions in the work, kingly and heroic love affairs especially being shown as conducted on an almost bourgeois level of respectability, as when the mighty hero Rustam, being assured of the passionate love of the beautiful Tahmina, sends for a Magian priest to perform the marriage ceremony before taking her to himself. And for gallantry there is the story of the Sasanian king Sapor (Shapur), who, after a successful day in the hunting field with his retinue, comes upon a prosperous-looking village surrounded by gardens and fields. He dismounts at the headman's house, which has a beautiful garden within its boundary wall, and enters the green and refreshing spot.

There he saw a maiden lovely as the moon, who had let a
    bucket down by the roller into the well.
When that beauteous maid beheld the face of Sapor,
    she approached and gave him greetings,
Saying, May you be blessed! May you be happy and glad!
    May you everlastingly be free of harm!
And now, without doubt, your horse must be athirst,
    and in this village the water is all brackish.
Yet in this well the water's very cool and sweet;
    permit me to be your drawer of water.
To her answered Sapor, "Beauteous maiden,
    why trouble yourself to talk in this way?
I have a servant here to wait upon me
    who will draw up the cool water from the well."
The maiden turned her face away from the youth,
    withdrew, and sat down by the garden brook.
His servant then the king commanded
    to bring a pail and draw up water from the well.
The man obeyed and came in haste.
    There was a rope upon the pail and the roller ran smooth.
When the bucket in the well was filled with water,
    the servant's face began to writhe [with effort]

73

Because the weighty pail would not come up from the well.
   Swiftly to him came King Shapur chiding;
Saying to the man, "Half-woman!
   did not the woman handle this bucket, roller, and rope?
She drew up great quantity of water from the well,
   while you are full distressed and call for help."
He advanced and took the rope from his servitor;
   but the task proved toilsome to the prince;
And when he found such trouble from the heavy pail
   he lavished praises on the beauteous maid
For having lifted a bucket of such weight.
   "Surely [said he], she is of royal stock."
When he drew up the bucket thus, the maid advanced
   and with kindness lavished praises on him.

A long sequence of verses is devoted in the *Shahnama*
to the romantic tale, of a *Romeo and Juliet* order, in which
Manizha, daughter of Afrasiyab, king of Turan, catches
sight of Bizhan, son of an Iranian warrior-prince, in the
hunting field and falls in love with him. She calls out to
him, introduces him secretly into her father's palace,
where she conceals him. A dramatic moment in the story
comes when Garsiwaz, brother of Afrasiyab and guardian
of the palace, discovers the intruder.

As Garsiwaz approached the gateway, from the hall there
   issued loud voices and the noise of drinking and eating,
The plucking of harps and the strumming of rebecks,
   emerging from Afrasiyab's hall.
Mounted men held the gateway and the [flat] roof of the royal
   hall, barring the way on every side.
When Garsiwaz saw that the palace gate was closed
   and that the wine and tumult and drinking continued,
He put out his hand and dislodged the fastening,
   then sprang from the gateway into the courtyard.
Swiftly he came to the mansion
   into which the stranger had intruded.

74

And when from the doorway his eye fell upon Bizhan,
  his blood boiled within him in his rage.
In that chamber were three hundred servitors
  all seated with rebecks, wine, and music,
While Bizhan sat amongst the women,
  at his lips red wine, making merry.
Seeing it Garsiwaz in his fury shouted out,
  "Shameless and unclean creature,
You have fallen into the clutch of a ravening lion;
  how will you escape from the midst of us here?"
In agony Bizhan within him thought,
  "How shall I give battle with my body naked?
Neither have I my night-black steed nor any swift mount;
  surely the Sun today has turned against me.
Where are Giw, and Gudarz, and the Kashwads [heroes]?
  Now surely I must sell my head for nothing.
In the whole world I see none to aid me;
  save God alone none is my ally."
But ever, along one leg within his boot,
  he bore a dagger of tempered steel.
He stretched out his hand, plucked the weapon from its sheath,
  put his back to the door and cried out his name.
"I am Bizhan," he called, "son of the Kashwads,
  prince of warriors and of free men.
Will none venture his skin against me?
  Like a clove of garlic his body would part from his head.
And were Resurrection to burst upon the world,
  none would behold my back in flight."

In the end Bizhan is seized, Afrasiyab casts him into a
pit and drives Manizha from his doors. By begging and
working at the humblest of tasks, she earns enough to
keep Bizhan supplied with food in his dungeon, until
Rustam appears on the scene with his army, releases the
captive, and takes him with his betrothed back to Iran.

No author could have embarked on a work as lengthy
as the *Shahnama* with a clear picture in his mind of how

it should run from the first word to the last. References which Firdausi makes to his age in various parts show that the episodes were not composed in the order in which they now appear but at times convenient to the poet, being then set down and linked by some fairly obvious literary contrivances. These consist of regular formulas introducing and concluding each story, with the result that we are reminded of the panoramas of the prephotographic age which, as they were unrolled piecemeal, displayed separate and detached aspects of life familiar to the audience from experience or hearsay.

Although we gain from the work a very good idea of what existence under the Sasanians was like, yet it remains in essence a product of the Samanid-Ghaznawid period, when princes and governors were rich and all-powerful, while those subject to them had to find their living as best they could. Firdausi, although pretending to describe historical conditions, clearly had contemporary circumstances in mind when he said:

> The toil comes from one, the fruit goes to another;
>   to justice or noblesse no one pays heed.
> Forgot is each promise, all turn from what's right,
>   the honors accrue to what's crooked and wrong.
> The fighter is thrown from his horse to the ground,
>   the braggart instead to the saddle is raised.
> Ploughman and soldier go poor and unheeded;
>   neither birth nor old age ever gets its desert.
>
>   .   .   .
>
> To plunder their neighbors and gain all themselves
>   is what men desire, using God as excuse.

It must be emphasized that Firdausi did not invent the legends and myths incorporated in the *Shahnama;* he was not a writer of fiction. The heroes—Rustam and Isfandiyar, Giw and Suhrab, Bizhan and Faridun as well as

76

the princesses they wooed and possessed—the demons, the monsters, and the fabulous animals had all been in popular currency from very ancient times. He put their adventures into verse based on Persian prose translations from Middle Persian or Pehlevi, using his imagination to provide plausible details, to invent lively descriptions of battles and triumphal banquets, to compose the lengthy speeches he put into the mouths of his characters and the numerous letters they sent to each other. Occasionally there is an unmistakable effort at rationalizing a legend, as when, at the conclusion of his tale of a combat between Rustam and a wicked Demon, he comments:

> The evil Demon here is the man who works ill,
>   he that refuses to follow the law of God.
> Should any man stray from the way of humanity,
>   then count him a Demon deserving God's wrath.

In his attitude towards religion Firdausi entered consistently into the feelings of the heroes who belonged to the ancient faith of Zoroastrianism, the expression of his views being unimpeded by the necessity which arose in later days to conceal any nonconformist beliefs and to comply with the theological doctrines imposed by orthodoxy and political authority. In his day Sufism had hardly begun to make its influence widely felt, so that the language of the *Shahnama* is free of the mystical obscurity in which the language of poetry in the centuries following Firdausi's era is veiled. He was accused of Shiism by the Sunnis because he showed sympathy for the claims of the Prophet's own family to the caliphate, but in fact he held firmly to the traditional doctrine that state and religion needed each other's support. No fanatic in belief, he may be regarded as one of the world's humanists. Indeed the great Sufi poet Maulavi Jalal al-Din, who lived about two-and-a-half centuries later, criticized him on the

77

ground that he was interested in fables that symbolized the husk of matters only, to the neglect of the kernel of reality, and rebuked an admirer of the *Shahnama* for profanely placing it and the *Fables of Bidpai* on a level with the Koran.

On literary grounds there have been few serious criticisms from sources in Persia, where the attitude towards Firdausi and his work is, understandably, one of admiration for an unexcelled national poet. Yet M. A. Furughi, a modern Persian literary historian, has pointed out how frequently in the *Shahnama* the same language is repeated in different circumstances. Battle scenes in particular are liable to be described with little change of incident or vocabulary, events in later parts of the work contradict what has been said in earlier portions, and little check is kept upon the comings and goings of the heroes.

By modern standards and to Western taste, the prime hindrances to enjoyment of the *Shahnama* or, let it be said, of any epics or sagas, are the archaic nature of their contents and language, their frequent repetitions, and the stereotyped nature of their characters. But such elements are part of the very stuff of epics and sagas. They were meant to be recited, as the *Shahnama* still is, and before enthusiastic audiences. Such poetry can only be composed if the poet has at his command a ready-made stock of traditional and familiar phrases, half-lines and lines, which he can throw in when he is at a loss for the precise words he needs. Since he composes while reciting, he must have on the tip of his tongue phrases of the right meter, and further, the use of rhyme keeps the audience in expectation of what is to come once the line has been started. So it is that standard qualifications, similes, and metaphors become associated in the poet's mind with certain types of persons and situations. Examples could be quoted from other literatures, but Falstaff in Shakespeare

78

and Micawber in Dickens are sufficiently familiar instances of characters who always arrive on the scene accompanied, or preceded, by their own special aura.

Exaggerated hyperbole, far-fetched tropes, and rhetorical overornamentation are other points that attract criticism. They are of course brought in by the poet to provide an atmosphere of boundless magnificence for his heroes, but they tend too often to fall into stereotyped molds. Thus, armies are almost always so vast that the wind cannot get by them, the dust of battle covers the sun and turns day into night, the tread of armed men flattens the hills, and a cavalry charge splits the earth apart, while in every town the king beholds a castle whose pinnacles reach higher than Saturn. Rustam's horse Rakhsh is so keen sighted that on a dark night he can see an ant crawling on a piece of black felt at a distance of two leagues, and a messenger sent on an errand does not delay even to scratch his head. Sunrise and sunset are always accompanied by elaborate and standardized similes. As for young women, their mouths are so small that their breath scarcely passes, their figures are tall slim cypresses, their eyes resemble the narcissus, and their faces are lovely as the moon at its full.

In the construction of so long a poem difficulties were unavoidably encountered in dovetailing the parts together. There are about fifty different episodes described, each with its introductory and concluding formula, but the verbal links by which they are connected receive the same treatment of meter and rhyme as the principal poems. There is no sharpening of detail for the main incidents to distinguish them from the transitional parts, and the machinery which should be artistically concealed remains in full view. In the poet's defense it must be said that he was bound by tradition and the poetical conventions imposed upon him. It was obviously impossible for a

79

lengthy composition which contains history, descriptions of battles, feasts and scenery, love passages, laments and even satire to retain interest at full stretch while the author was restricted to a single meter. The very regularity of it was bound to produce a monotony. Nevertheless, the *Shahnama*, even as it stands, can hold its own with the national classics of other peoples. In the Islamic world it is unique.

Exactly when the *Shahnama* was completed is a matter of some speculation, because although in one passage Firdausi tells us that he put the last touches to the work in the four-hundredth year of the Hegira, equivalent to 1009–1010, in another he indicates that it was ready sixteen years earlier. It is probable that the earlier version was a first draft meant to be presented to the warrior Sultan Mahmud of Ghazna. The intermediary between author and sultan was to have been the chief minister Abu'l-'Abbas Isfara'ini, but he seems to have fallen out of favor before he could be of service to the poet, who waited in vain for the reward he thought was his due for his achievement. Firdausi was poor and ill when at last he found a generous patron, by which time, as he bitterly complained, copies of his work had been made for all the rich and powerful in the land, who got it for nothing. A famous satire included in the *Shahnama* proclaims that if Mahmud had not had a slave for his father, he would have known how to deal like a free, and freehanded, man towards a poet who had brought him fame.

The traditional materials turned to such grandiose effect by Firdausi were in part used again by the poet Nizami (Jalal al-Din Ilyas ibn Yusuf) of Ganja, a city of the Caucasus identifiable with the present Kirovabad in Soviet Azarbaijan. When he was born and when he died is, characteristically, a matter of dispute among the biographers, but it is certain that he flourished in the second half of the twelfth century. What assures him of a place in the upper levels of Persian literature is his mastery of the art of erotic verse, his efforts in that genre being incorporated in the five long romantic and dramatic mathnavi poems known collectively in Persian as *Panj Ganj* (*Five Treasures*), but more often by the Arabic title of the *Khamsa* (*Quintet*).

Nizami's use of the ancient legends differs from Firdausi's in his laying emphasis rather on the human than on the superhuman, or heroic, aspects of his characters. He is perhaps also more truly a poet than his better-known predecessor, in that, like Shakespeare or Goethe, he looked upon the world with eyes undimmed by preconceived ideas. Firdausi, as a loyal son, regarded Iran as the hub of the universe and anyone who trespassed upon its interests as an enemy or traitor. Similarly the authors of the didactical mathnavis began their work in an attitude which favored certain beliefs or principles and were inclined to regard the phenomena of life as so many facts supporting their own theories. Nizami set things down as his reason saw them, without patriotic, religious, or mystical bias.

Nizami's most notable characteristic as a craftsman is his skill in the use of imagery and metaphor, mastery in which is said to distinguish great poets from mere imitators. He was expert too in the way in which he could verbally animate the elements of a natural scene and make them behave in human style, much in the same way as cinema cartoonists can do it for the screen. Similes with him become the reality, the veritable things they are reflecting, and take on a life of their own. Thus: "The nenuphar's eye from the tight grip of sleep/escapes into the water's stronghold." Another example is this, depicting the dawn: "The sun, emerging from his azure fortress, / pitched his tents upon the walls of yellowness";

and again, on the same theme: "A thousand narcissi
[the stars] upon the world-encircling/wheel went under
so that one yellow [sun-] flower might come up." A
picture of nightfall is: "Night, [the moment] when this
exhausted phoenix [the world]/filled its belly with this
unique ruby [the sun]."

Most of the Five are full to excess of overelaborate
imagery of the kind. The plots, on the other hand, are as
a rule simple, deriving from the ancient national repertory.
The first, *The Treasury of Secrets*, does not altogether fit
in with the general scheme, being little more than a
mystical poem with illustrative anecdotes. The second,
Khusrau and Shirin, deals with the career of the Sasanian
king Khusrau Parwiz and more particularly concerns
his amorous adventures with the beautiful Armenian
Christian princess Shirin. Variety is added to the plot
by the intervention of the engineer Farhad as a rival for
the princess's affections. To test his love she gives him the
task of cutting a channel through the mountain of Bisitun,
by which water may be led to her castle of Qasr-i Shirin.
Khusrau is well aware of this scheme and in order to bring
the romance to an end sends a messenger to the engineer,
busily at work on his impossible task, with the false
information that Shirin had died. Broken hearted, the
wretched lover crashes headlong down the mountainside
to his death, leaving the king to enjoy his beloved's
favors without interruption. To the reader brought up in
the Western tradition, the lack of poetic justice comes as
a shock, but our Persian poet is a realist who sets his
materials down as though they were facts of ordinary
life. Yet the whole treatment of the poem is directed
towards glamor, and it is not so much the subject matter
that signifies as the beauty of the phraseology and the
rhythm of the language. There are metaphors in abundance to lend color to the language of the verse, with

similes and other figures of speech so numerous and elaborate that the action can for the most part scarcely be seen
moving.

Laili and Majnun, the next mathnavi, is a tragic poem
in the tradition of courtly love that tells how the beautiful
Laili, married by her father for his own purposes to a
husband she does not love, pines for the affection of
Majnun (the distracted), who had been the companion
of her schooldays. He for his part, driven out of his mind
by hopeless passion, takes refuge in the desert, where he
makes friends with the untamed creatures that roam the
wastes and that become the confidants of his woes. After
a period of time, Laili's husband dies, and, the obstacles
to their union being now removed, she invites Majnun
to visit her. When the lover arrives and they are at last
alone together, able to open their hearts, they discover
that their long separation has made them strangers. To
her he now appears to be without a life and ambition of
his own, his one desire being to merge with her and be
her shadow, while to him she appears to be hard and
lacking in sympathy. In the depths of disillusionment he
hastens back to the wilderness and the companionship
of beasts, amongst whom, however, he soon dies. With his
departure, life loses its meaning for Laili and shortly
afterward she follows him to the grave.

Fourth of the Five comes the *Bahram-nama* (Book of
Bahram) or, more commonly, the *Haft Paikar* (The Seven
Portraits), from a series of stories that make up the majority
of the work. It is one of the last of Nizami's mathnavis
and is not so greatly "pestered with metaphor" as some of
the others, the action being less seriously impeded by
description. In outward form the *Haft Paikar* consists of
a framework story—ostensibly the life, more specifically
the love life, of the Sasanian king Bahram Gur (Bahram
the Wild Ass, alluded to in FitzGerald's *Ruba'iyat*)—in

83

which are embedded a number of anecdotes mostly of a fairy-tale character. After the customary pious invocations and the dedications to royal patrons, the mathnavi begins by relating how Bahram was brought up in Hira, an Arab kingdom owing allegiance to the Sasanians. There he achieved fame as a horseman and mighty hunter who, when he was not in pursuit of game, was occupied in wine-bibbing.

> His horse could outpace the wind by a stage,
> Its tail curled like a hundred serpents,
> Its hoofs dug the graves of a hundred wild asses.

A promising beginning is made in the first inset story by Bahram's discovery of a secret locked chamber as he wandered one day about the palace. After a search for a missing chamberlain with the key, the door was opened and there, painted upon the walls, were the pictures of seven beautiful maidens, each a princess from one of the Seven Climes of the habitable world. Over them was an inscription mentioning the name of Bahram Gur and declaring that when this world-conqueror made his appearance he would clasp these seven maidens like seven pearls to his royal bosom. In wonderment at the workings of destiny, he fell promptly in love with the delineaments of these imperial charmers, the scene, as the poet earthily describes it, being of "mares in heat and a stallion at their service / A young lion of a man with a septet of brides."

When Bahram had in due course succeeded to his father's throne and made himself master of his empire, he summoned the kings of the Seven Climes to send him the maidens with whom he had fallen in love. For each he built a splendid dome-capped mansion dedicated to its own planet and adorned in its own symbolical color. He visits each in turn on her own day of the week, when she tells him a story to entertain him, the stories

84

collectively making up the main body of the work. But
there is an interlude in the framework story which is a great
favorite. It tells how Fitna (mischief), Bahram's favorite
slave girl, who was his chosen companion at both his
hunting and his wine-bibbing, once challenged him in the
field to pin together the ear and the hoof of a wild ass
with a single arrow. He rose to the occasion by shooting
a pellet at the beast's ear and then, when it put up its
hoof to allay the irritation, letting fly an arrow. It is a
scene often pictured by the miniature-painters.

Fitna, overestimating her powers of fascination, instead of paying the prince the compliment he anticipated
merely scoffed at his skill as something which anyone
might acquire with practice. This impertinence sent him
into such a rage that he ordered her instant execution.
But the officer to whom the order was given, as usual in
such stories, was softened by her loveliness and failed to
carry out his duty. Instead he took her into hiding in a
remote village where he had a noble mansion, one feature
of which was a lofty portico with a flat roof only to be
reached by a flight of sixty steps. Here the maiden spent
most of her time, getting exercise each day by carrying
up a young calf which was born after her arrival. In the
course of time, the calf grew into a bull. Fitna then con-
spired with her protector to induce the prince to come
hunting in the neighborhood, when he could be invited into
the mansion and, after a suitable feast, she might find the
opportunity of showing what could be done with practice.

That Nizami was capable of better things than so trite
and long-winded a story he demonstrated in the allegory
of Mahan, another interlude in the *Bahram-nama*. It is
a story with a moral, almost in the nature of Bunyan's
Pilgrim's Progress, which tells how the hero Mahan, after
he had passed through one scene after another—either
wilderness or garden of bliss, but all alike peopled by the

demons of temptation and lust—won through at last to salvation. Beginning on a beautiful moonlit night in an Egyptian garden, where Mahan had been making merry with some friends, the tale recounts how, aglow with wine, he left the garden and entered deep into a palm grove in which he lost all direction. Suddenly a man appeared who claimed to be an old trading acquaintance.

"I have come," he said, "from a far journey, and my
   heart could not rest without seeing you.
I have brought profits beyond reckoning, so much that
   I must thank God for them.
When I reached the city it was late; the gate was closed
   and my house not to be reached.

        .   .   .

But it is possible now, while the night is dark, to hide
   half the money and escape the taxes."

Mahan, his cupidity aroused, accompanied his friend at a rapid pace, until it occurred to him that they should long before have reached the Nile, which was not a league distant from the garden, whereas they had walked four leagues or more without coming to it. Feeling themselves lost they hesitated, going "slowly back, then swiftly forward." A bird called, and suddenly it was dawn. As Mahan looked about him he realized that his companion had vanished. Anxious and weary now he lay down on the ground, and was only wakened when the sun was high in the heavens. The scene that met his eyes was terrifying; all around him were caves, and the mouth of each was guarded by a serpent more awful than a dragon.

Although no strength remained in his legs, his mind told him he must go on. Night fell again, "and every blade of grass became in his eyes a serpent." In the abode of demons through which he wandered next he heard a human voice, and as he looked he saw two persons approaching, a man and a woman, each laden with a heavy bundle. Said the man, "Who are you, and how did you come to this place of solitude where is no human habitation? Demons live here." Mahan answered, "Someone brought me here who told me he was my partner in profits and goods. When daylight came he disappeared."

"You have escaped by a hair," said the other. "That was a demon, and when he spoke to you of money his purpose was to destroy your soul. But this woman and I are your friends; we will watch over you tonight." All night he walked on between them, no one uttering a word. And then, as dawn broke, "a cock's crow came like a drumbeat," a village stood before them, and his two companions vanished through the gate.

Again Mahan resumed his perilous journey, this time through a wild and rocky pass. As he sat resting by the mouth of a cave, a man riding one horse and leading another approached and halted in front of him, asking him what he did there. Mahan again told his story and the man remarked, "Those were two ghouls. They carry men off the road, cast them into a cave and shed their blood. If the cry of birds comes to them, they flee. Make haste. Mount my spare horse, keep a tight rein and speak no word, good or ill."

Mounting into the saddle, Mahan followed his guide through a rocky mountain defile, from which they descended into a flat plain where all about them they kept hearing strains of music and the sound of voices calling to them. Some said "Come this way!" others called out "Happy drinking to you!" Everywhere thousands of torches blazed and the whole plain was filled with ghouls clapping hands, dancing and shouting. Monstrous figures with the trunks of elephants and the horns of oxen approached the two horsemen; tongues of flame issued from their throats while they recited verses, keeping time to the rhythm by combing their hair. Soon the whole world was dancing. Mahan's horse, moving with dainty steps, joined in with the rest, and as he looked down at it in wonder he beheld that wings were sprouting from its legs and that beneath him were terror and destruction, for he was now mounted on a dragon, which had four legs and two wings and, more amazing still, seven heads.

His terrible mount leaped about with him until morning came and then flung him to the ground, where he lay stunned and senseless until the sun's heat roused him to consciousness. He rubbed his eyes and, raising himself to his feet, continued his journey. It led him this time through a deserted land whose air was so miasmic that an arrow lingered in passage through it. He came at last to a town that showed no sign of life, and entered a lane which held a deep well. A thousand steps led down to the bottom, and though his legs were now as slack as pieces of rope he descended to quench his thirst, and then slept. As he looked up from his sleep, he saw that the well gleamed like a new silver piece and the whole place was bright with moonshine that came through a crack in the side. With his nails and fingers he tore open the crack until it was wide enough to let his head and then his body pass through. He found himself in a pleasant garden, studded with trees bearing fruits of every kind, from pomegranates like caskets of rubies to pistachio nuts opening in a smile. Of all these he ate his fill.

As he was eating he heard a loud voice cry out, "Seize the robber!" and out came an enraged old man carrying a cudgel. "Who are you, and what do you do here?" he demanded. Humbly and in terror Mahan replied, "I am a stranger, far from home. Show kindness to a wanderer who has seen much suffering." At that the old man laid down his stick and listened to Mahan's story, from the time of his setting out to the moment when he found himself in that garden of delights.

When Mahan had concluded his tale, the old man said, "Those creatures were demons. They profess to guide men on the right path but deal crookedly with them; they take men by the hand, but cast them into the pit. The key to verity is that it is everlasting; that is what distinguishes the true miracle from wizardry. Those fantasies came into your mind because of the simplicity of your soul; they attacked you because your going astray had troubled your conscience."

The homily is followed by Mahan's being introduced into a paradise "before the Resurrection of the dead," but even as he is enjoying the sensual embraces of one of its voluptuous houris he finds her turning into a monster and the whole of his paradise transformed into a hell. He has once again been deluded by smooth and specious words, "unaware that every possession of ours, being veiled in moonshine, is naught but a chimaera." Thereafter Mahan is permitted to come to his sober self again and to follow the path of true virtue.

The *Bahram-nama* ends on a dramatic note with the disappearance of Bahram, while on a hunting expedition, into a cleft in some rocks from which he never issues again. "None believed that the Elephant of that Pleasant Land had seen a vision and returned to his native Hindustan."

The last of the five mathnavis, the *Iskandar-nama*, is also the longest, running to more than ten thousand lines. It deals with those more or less fabulous incidents in the career of Alexander the Great that Firdausi had omitted from the *Shahnama*, but it also expatiates on his universal knowledge and his wisdom.

In the second of the two parts into which the *Iskandar-nama* is divided, there occurs an adaptation of the classical legend which gave rise to the saying that, when the breezes stir the reeds, they whisper, "King Midas has the ears of an ass." According to Muslim tradition Iskandar was called *Zu'l-Qarnain,* "The Two-Horned." How he earned the appellation is disputed, but one basis for it is that the king had the long ears of an ass, and in connection with that, Nizami has a story to tell. Iskandar, says the poet, covered these ears with a circlet of pearls as protection for them and to guard them from the sight of men, so that none but the slave who acted as his barber had any knowledge of them.

But this man passed from the world and left the need for another barber. A new craftsman in the barber's art came, and in confidence the secret was disclosed to him. While the conqueror's hair was being dressed one day, he said softly to the man, "If it comes to my ears that anyone has carried the story of these jewel-decked ears of mine to other ears, I will in vengeance give your ears such a rubbing that you will never again say what must not be said."

The man departed, after placing the ring of obedience in his ear. He forgot not those words alone but his very tongue and spoke of that matter to no one in the world, keeping it concealed in his heart as close as misbelief. But from the effort of concealment his face grew sallow, for hiding a secret brings pain to the heart. One day he stealthily left the palace in his distress and came to a wide open plain where he beheld a great cave in which was a deep well. Into the well he cast the report that the king of the world had exceedingly long ears. With the utterance of the words, his heart emptied itself of all its care. Slowly he went back home, guarding the seal upon his tied tongue.

It was heard thereafter that out of that deep well, in harmony with the man's sorrowful note, a reed had grown.

It raised its head out of the well and reached upwards, but the hand of a thief stretched out to the treasure. A shepherd from the wilderness passed that way and, seeing the reed growing out of the depths of the well, plucked it and, as is the practice of shepherds, made a pipe of it, first cutting it then playing upon it. He troubled his heart little with thought, but with the reed he kept it happy.

One day the king went out into the open lands about the town and there he passed by an ancient shepherd. He caught sight of the reed which from afar he had heard the shepherd playing, and the world became confused in his eyes, for in the reed's fluting he had heard the secret words: "Iskandar has two long ears." So hot did he become at the reed's murmur that steel melted in his wrath. For long he stamped about inwardly debating, but came to no decision. He called the shepherd to him, keeping the secret of himself hidden, and the man openly told him the story of the reed. Amazement fell upon the king at this narration. Making his way homewards he seated himself in his private quarters and summoned the barber. To him he said, "Man of feeble judgment, you who reveal matters covered up; to whom did you divulge my secret and into whose ear did you inject the story? If you tell me, you are free of fetters and sword; otherwise, with hot irons and tongs your head shall be removed."

The barber heard the words and saw no course better than to tell the truth. But first he swept the dust of the path with his eyelashes, uttered blessings, and then said, "When your Majesty charged me with the trust of keeping veiled the brides in their cradle, my heart was pierced through by the secret. The story was breathed down a well; I told it to no living soul, O Lord of good counsel. If I did, may God be my enemy!"

91

When the king heard the man's heart-penetrating secret, he sought proof of the words. He ordered a trusty courtier to fetch from the well a fluting reed, which, when a breath found a passage into its depth, uttered that very secret to the king. He perceived that in the whole range of worldly concerns nothing that any man wishes to be kept hidden may remain for ever concealed.

The Five Treasures taken together must be regarded as achieving a high standard by any literary criterion, for there lies in them a great store of poetic imagination displaying an abundance of glamorous pictures. Their fault is that all is too rich, too dazzling in imagery, so that the mind turns for relief to something sober and less glittering.

FIVE : PERSIAN MYSTICS

Before considering the next of the great classical poets of Persia, namely "Maulavi" (or "Mevlevi," as the title is pronounced in Turkish) Jalal al-Din Rumi, something more requires to be said about the beliefs and attitude towards life which inspired his work. Ritual, or "outward" celebration in fulfillment of prescribed duties, had never satisfied the spiritual longings of all Muslims. When the Arab Umayyads by use of the strong hand built up a mighty empire, many who felt the weight of their oppression sought refuge in "other worldliness," finding little guidance in the laws laid down by the doctors of the faith, who demanded from the faithful no more than worship, payment of the alms tax, fasting, and pilgrimage and left it to each believer to seek his own peace with God. Some, like human beings everywhere, found the problems of life in general lacking a rational solution or felt the demands of society beyond their power to bear. Mysticism was the resort for them and those others for whom orthodoxy and conformity were insufficient.

Here and there men arose with the power to give

expression to their inward aspirations and unhappy longings, or who indicated a path which would lead to quietude and spiritual solace. The movement of dissatisfaction that had begun with manifestations in Syria and Iraq received enthusiastic support in the eastern Persian province of Khurasan, where the Umayyad tyranny had been heavy. In the earlier days of the spiritual revolt the framework of orthodox Islam had not become as rigid as its legists afterward insisted that it should be, and it remained susceptible to influences and modifications from its environment. In Syria the new faith of Islam had grown up in a land where Christian monasteries of various orders had long been established, while both Khurasan and Transoxiana were the homes of flourishing Buddhist communities. These showed that a self-denying way of life and a disregard of material prosperity could be at one and the same time a religion and a form of revolt against authority. Furthermore there were the adherents of asceticism, a negative virtue, which associated affliction of the body with the anxiety brought on by a sense of transgression of divine commands and a primitive fear of retribution.

The mystical "otherworldliness" to which these various people adhered became known in its Muslim environment as "Sufism," a term derived from the Arabic word *suf* (wool), a coarse variety of which material was used for the making of the rough, patched cloak worn as a sign of their brotherhood by those in the movement. "Sufism" is not identical with "mysticism" but is a term applied to that form of it which had its origins in the environment of Islam. Its one and only central idea— there being no single school of doctrine with fixed tenets— was that of the Oneness of the universe. It led directly to pantheism, and this according to Muslim orthodoxy was sheer heresy that normally demanded concealment.

94

When therefore the Sufi Mansur al-Hallaj (The Wool carder) came to the logical conclusion—uttered in public —that since everything was God, he too was "Reality" (or God), he was hanged as a misbeliever.

The Reality the Sufis spoke of was the Divine Essence, which manifested itself in the world of phenomena and was "immanent" in it, but was also "transcendental," as above and beyond all phenomena. Not merely, said they, is there "no God but Allah," as the orthodox declared, but there is nothing at all but God. The two concepts had to be reconciled if Sufis were to continue in Islam, and the task was performed in scholastic fashion by the Persian theologian Ghazali about the end of the eleventh century. He did it by dwelling on Koranic texts and Prophetic traditions which might be interpreted as having mystical significance and omitting from his expositions those passages which had an opposing tendency.

It was part of Sufi teaching that an important element in the universe created by God in order that He "should be known" was Man, in whom He placed a spark of himself, although with "the penalty of body" attached to it. Man's duty is to wear away the body, "to die to self," in order that the spark within him may be united, and remain permanently with, the One Reality or Truth. That is the basic assumption of Sufi mysticism.

When speaking of these mysteries the poets and expositors of *tasawwuf*, the Arabic term normally used for Sufism, were hampered by the inadequacies of human language. The Truth, which is transcendental Reality, cannot be compassed even by thought, let alone speech, and the only means of conveying a glimpse of its significance to man's restricted sense and reason is by metaphor and allegory. "Metaphor is a bridge to Reality," say the Sufis. Shakespeare, when he bejeweled his work with word-painting such as "how sweet the moonlight sleeps upon that bank," was referring to things which human beings could see for themselves. The Sufi poet, dealing entirely with immaterial concepts, was compelled to use his experience of passionate emotions to indicate, however vaguely, what he wished to convey.

Sufi symbolism turns about the pivotal points of Love, Wine, and Beauty, for the only means the mystical poet has of conveying some hint of union with the Divine is in human terms. His language therefore sometimes transgresses religious and moral prescriptions, in view of his avowed toleration of beliefs and practices frowned upon by those who could lay down the law. As used by him, such terms as "Love," "Wine," "Tavern," "Cup," "Cup-bearer," "Saki," and the like are, he claims, to be used in the mystical sense. Thus the tavern is the place where "Believer and Armenian, Zoroastrian, Christian, and Jew" receive and drink the Wine of Unity handed out by the "Taverner," the "Elder of the Magians," the "Guide," whose assistant, the "Saki" (the "Wine-server"), takes round the cups.

Love is the intoxication of the Wine of Unity and is an intimation of the Divine, or rather, only the shadow of the Divine. This love is intensified by music and dancing, which heighten the fervor leading to mystical ecstasy by making the "ear of the soul" receptive, until the moment comes when an intimation of Unity may be attained. Here reason is excluded as being the antithesis of love, with which rational conduct is incompatible. Some indication of what this implies may be gained from a passage of the *Bustan* (*The Scented Garden*) of Sa'di of Shiraz, a younger contemporary of Jalal al-Din's.

If you are a man of Love, take the path of self-loss—
or else choose safety.

Fear not Love's turning you to dust; by its annihilating
    you, you become everlasting.
That will give you the acquaintanceship with the Real
    which will give you deliverance from the clutch of Self.
For being with Self you find no way into your inward Self;
    only the selfless understand this subtlety.
Not minstrelsy but the rhythm of horses' hooves
    is music, if you have love and a soul in turmoil.

.   .   .

When they who are in exaltation perform their wine-worship,
    they are intoxicated by the creaking of a waterwheel.
Like the waterwheel they begin to revolve,
    and like the waterwheel they shed bitter tears over themselves.

.   .   .

The world is filled with music, intoxication, and turbulence;
    But how can a blind man see in a looking glass?

SANA'I OF GHAZNA

The recognized masters of the Sufi didactic poetry that
was intended for the instruction and guidance of the
novice on the Mystic Path are Sana'i of Ghazna, who
flourished in the first half of the twelfth century; Farid
al-Din 'Attar ("the Druggist") of Nishapur, who died
about 1220; and "Maulavi" Jalal al-Din Rumi, who died
in 1273. The last is the greatest for the quality and extent
of his poetry, but he acknowledged his indebtedness
to the first two in the lines: "'Attar was the spirit
and Sana'i its two eyes: / I followed on Sana'i and 'Attar."
    Sana'i was a pioneer in the genre of the didactic
mathnavi composed on Sufi themes. Few exact biographical details are preserved about him. The year neither of
his birth nor of his death is known, and he has been
ascribed indifferently to Nishapur and Balkh, both in

the old province of Khurasan. What may be told with
certainty is that he acted as court poet to the Ghaznavid
sultan Bahram Shah in the second quarter of the twelfth
century. He was author of a large collection of poems,
both qasidas and ghazals, in addition to several mathnavis,
of which the most famous and most esteemed in Persia
is that which goes under the title of *Hadiqat al-Haqiqa*
(*The Garden of Truth*). It contains ten chapters, which, in
not very polished style, cover some aspects of Sufism.

FARID AL-DIN 'ATTAR

Following him in time as a mathnavi writer came Farid
al-Din 'Attar, a man of much greater versatility and
writing skill. He was a native of Nishapur, one of the
Khurasan capitals, and lost his life there, probably in
1220 when the Mongols under Chingiz Khan overran
the city. So many works have been ascribed to him, with
such great incompatibilities of style and contents amongst
them, that they convey the impression that some at least
were not written by him. However that may be, there
is agreement that the best known and most accomplished
are of his authorship. They are the *Mantiq al-Tair* (*The
Language of the Birds*), the *Ilahi-nama* (*The Book of Saints*),
and the *Musibat-nama* (*The Book of Travail*), all three
mystical mathnavis consisting of a framework poem that
carries a story, with anecdotes inserted at frequent intervals to illustrate points that arise. These anecdotes in
themselves make a storehouse of Persian folklore, ranging
from the grim to the comic, with any number of gradations
in between but all directed towards conveying a moral.

The Language of the Birds is a long allegorical mathnavi
which describes how the birds go in search of the Simurgh,
the mythical creature in the form of a bird who represents
"Reality" or God. The story opens with the assembly

of the birds, the hoopoe with his crown being leader because he had once been King Solomon's emissary to the Queen of Sheba. He addresses them on the need to go in quest of the Simurgh, but declares that the way promises to be long and difficult. At that each begins to make his excuses. The nightingale pleads that he is engaged all night long in repeating his songs of love, that lovers could not dispense with him, and that he himself could not be parted from his beloved, the rose. The parrot with his green robe and crown of gold explains that he is kept in a cage of iron, from which he could not gain release.

Then comes the peacock, each feather ornamented, to reveal how his unfortunate association with the Serpent and the expulsion from the Garden of Eden, has made him unworthy to share in this journey. The duck says that, being the cleanest of fowls, he could not go without water; the red-billed partridge cannot separate himself from the jewel-filled quarries in the mountains; the *huma*, who provides shade for kings, cannot abrogate his function, nor can the hawk leave the royal hand. The heron declares himself a harmless, melancholy bird who stands contemplatively at the river's brink all day and cannot travel. The owl, the sparrow, and all the other birds similarly have their reasons for not undertaking the arduous pilgrimage. *154526*

To all their objections the hoopoe makes convincing replies, and then, finding that they must go, the birds suddenly realize that they are related to the Simurgh and are eager to be off. Their leader now warns them again of the difficulties they must undergo on the Sufi Path and then leads them through the Seven Valleys of Seeking, Love, Gnosis, Self-reliance, Acknowledgment of One-ness, Uncertainty, and, lastly, Destitution and Death to Self. In the end they discover the Simurgh, and in so doing discover themselves.

The *Ilahi-nama* (*The Book of Saints*) tells the story of a king who had six sons, from each of whom in turn he demanded to know what his dearest wish was. The first and eldest desired to wed the beautiful daughter of the king of the peris.

"That," said the father, "is a token of sensuality. Far better would it be for you to marry a loving and faithful wife who will provide you with children. In any event, the object of your passion is only the creation of your own spirit, and there you will find her."

The second son wished to acquire the art of magic, which would enable him to wander about the world in every possible guise, take possession of anything that took his fancy, and so become lord of the world. The king's answer was that magic was the evil work of Satan.

To own the magic cup of Jamshid and so learn all the world's secrets mirrored in it was the third son's wish. His father discouraged him by replying that the wish was dictated by ambition and eagerness to feel superior to the rest of mankind. The fourth son wanted the "Water of Everlasting Life," but was told it was only because he looked forward excessively to the accumulation of wealth. The fifth son's desire was to have Solomon's seal ring, which would gain him mastery over mankind and spirits and allow him to understand the language of the beasts and the birds. To that the father replied that kingship was transient and full of cares, hence undesirable.

The sixth and last of the princes expressed the unromantic desire to learn the art of making gold, supporting his request, however, with the argument that lack of gold led to irreligion and that since both the world and the faith were based on wealth it was lawful to pray to God for the Philosopher's Stone which would turn base metal into gold. That argument was demolished by the father, who tells how Plato, constructing the elixir out of the humblest materials, was able to make gold so easily that it became as valueless as dirt to him.

In the third of the major didactic poems of 'Attar, *The Book of Travail*, the meditative soul is personified as a novice of the Sufi Path undergoing a forty-day period of solitary retreat, which was a regular part of the novice's training. Each day he traversed one of the Stations of the Path, encountering in turn the Archangels; the divine Throne; the well-guarded Tablet on which the original of the Koran is preserved; the Pen which recorded all things to be; Paradise and Hell; the Heavens, Sun, and Moon; the Four Elements of Fire, Air, Earth, and Water; the animal, vegetable, and mineral constituents of the universe; and other phenomena. From each he receives instruction, at each step diversified by anecdotes drawn from many sides of life as lived in the small towns or villages of the author's period as well as from traditional legends. Here is one:

A clownish drunkard on a winter's night
  fell into the mire, his shoes in his hand.
Someone asked him, "Have you a mind for the road?
  Whither do you wish to go from here?"
He said, "I'm hasting to the burial ground;
  there's a sinner there being tormented.
That's where I'm going; his grave's full of fire.
  There I'll get warm, I find this cold unkind.
One man suffers death in that woeful way
  while for another death makes good provision.
Sin sets fire to your very being,
  casts you deep into mire and blood.

Another anecdote seems to betray the thought that Sufi doctrine was not always completely understood even by those who professed to teach it. It starts off by speaking of the vexation caused to a creditor by a debtor reluctant to pay what he owed. A dervish who intervened in the subsequent quarrel said to the creditor:

"The gold will be of greater use to you at Resurrection,
    resign it to him and go your way."
The plaintiff answered, "At Resurrection I from him
    clearly will not be able to claim the gold.
Tomorrow he will not hold his peace for me,
    that is why I strive so much with him today."
Said the dervish, "I don't see the secret of that.
    Explain it and make the obscurity clear."
He answered, "When we two emerge from the cage [of the
    flesh],
    He and I become one, and no more than that.
At the time when God shall 'One-ness' proclaim,
    for there to be 'Two-ness' would be heresy then.
Since in 'Reality' I'll be he and he I,
    surely my adversary he would not be.
Here below, however, no 'One-ness' is seen;
    I'll press my claim, and find use for the gold."

There 'Attar leaves the problem, but Jalal al-Din, who followed him, would have found a solution or at least been able to point a moral.

JALAL AL-DIN RUMI

Jalal al-Din was born at Balkh in Khurasan, from which, not many years after his birth, the terrible shadow of the advancing Mongol hordes decided his father to emigrate. During the years when Jalal al-Din was growing to maturity, he and his parents were traveling on the high-roads, first to Mecca by way of Baghdad, then, after performing the Pilgrimage, northward to Damascus. They settled finally at Konia in Rum (Asia Minor)—for which reason Jalal al-Din is frequently entitled "Rumi" —where he came under the influence of a Sufi community, whose way of life he adopted. In course of time he achieved the position of Sheik ("elder") and the title of *maulana* ("our master"), from which derives his own name and that of the dervish order (*Maulavi, Mevlevi* in Turkish) he founded.

His ambition in life now was to approximate himself to the mystical condition of the Perfect (Ideal) Man in whom the divine qualities are so evident that the lover "realizes that he and his Beloved are not two but one." As preceptors to direct him towards this goal he at various times took a number of "spiritual guides," the most effective of them a mysterious personage who appears in the pages of Rumi's biography under the title of *Shams-i Tabriz* (*The Sun of Tabriz*). So completely did he merge his personality into this "other self" that in an enormous divan which he composed he substituted the pen name "Shams-i Tabriz" for his own. Part of one of the ghazals there incorporated bears on the question of wine and love and of the equivocal senses in which these terms may be understood:

Come Saki, hand me a cup of dark wine
    that in the Magian cloister I may perceive Reality.
Remorse I've cast aside, that in full contentment
    for a time I may sit happily at the tavern door.
I care nought for penitence, self-denial, or piety,
    now that I find my happiness there.
I'll throw off cant, pretense, and sanctimony
    and let the vat-house Saki draw deep draughts for me.
And when I drain the life-restoring cup he hands me,
    I'll shift the garb of abstinence and devotion from the
        cloister.
Come then, my beloved, leave your secluded chamber,
    that in your face my woeful heart may find its joy.
'Tis towards it that men of insight turn in their devotions;
    and should I divert my cheek, then have I lost my faith.

Contained within the *Divan-i Shams-i Tabriz* are two thousand or more odes, many revolving about the problem of mystic One-ness, an idea that generates a spirit of magnificent toleration which here and there results in a poem full of splendid vision. One of the finest was translated by the late Reynold Alleyne Nicholson. The words are simple, but their full flavor cannot be conveyed in a rendering which is necessarily without the music and rhyme of the original text. It is the human soul that speaks.

I was, on the day when the heavens were not;
    no hint was there that anything with a name existed.
Through us[1] named and names became apparent
    on the day when no "I" or "We" were there.
A hint came in the revelation of the tip of the Beloved's tress[2]
    when the tip of the Beloved's tress was not.
Cross and Christianity from end to end
    I traversed. He was not in the Cross.
To the idol-house I went, the ancient cloister;
    in that no tinge of it was perceptible.
I went to the mountain of Herat and Kandahar;
    I looked. He was not in the depths or the heights there.
With purpose I ascended to the summit of Mount Qaf;[3]
    in that place was nought but the ʻAnqa.[4]
I turned the reins of search towards the Kaʻba;[5]
    He was not in that place to which old and young aspire.
I questioned Avicenna[6] about him;
    He was not within Avicenna's range.
I journeyed to the scene of "the two bow-lengths' distance";[7]
    He was not in that sublime Court.
I looked into my own heart.
    There I saw him; He was nowhere else.

[1] I.e., Man.   [2] Phenomena.   [3] It compasses the earth.
[4] A fabulous bird regarded by Sufis as a symbol of the unknown Godhead.   [5] The Meccan shrine.
[6] The famous philosopher and physician renowned in the history of medicine.
[7] (Cf. Koran LIII, v. 8f.) The distance to which the archangel Gabriel approached the Prophet when delivering a Koranic revelation from Heaven.

Voluminous as was Jalal al-Din Rumi's output of "Shams-i Tabriz" ghazals, his chief and most widely influential work was the *Mathnavi-i Ma'navi*, or *Spiritual Mathnavi*, a veritable library or encyclopedia, albeit uncoordinated, of Sufi lore. It contains about twenty-five thousand lines divided into six "books," and is addressed to a favorite disciple named Husam al-Din, who came to sit at his feet after the disappearance of Shams-i Tabriz. Earlier Sufi mathnavis, such as *The Garden of Truth* by Sana'i and *The Language of the Birds* by Farid al-Din 'Attar of Nishapur, although pointing the way to Rumi's work, had been little more than edifying discourses in verse with anecdotes to enliven the homilies. Rumi covered the whole range of life and thought experienced by Sufis, not alone in Persia, which he had left as a boy, but in all Muslim lands, although his anecdotal passages usually have Iran as their background.

Here is the finest achievement of Persian mysticism, one which has, both in its original language and in translation, found a very wide public in Iran and outside of it. Addressed primarily to convinced Sufis, it yet does not reject literary devices designed to seize and hold the attention of unsophisticated audiences in stretches of exposition where there was a danger of their thoughts wandering. Anecdotes of every description are brought in, grave and gay, pious and bawdy, very often drifting along for many hundreds of lines until the thread of the discourse is lost and the story oozes away in the sands of mystic speculation. Hardly any sign appears of a plan or of systematic guidance in the practice of Sufism. Yet an occasional remark aside suggests that Rumi was not without method in his selection of materials and the use he made of them. "Listen," he says in one passage, "to the 'outward' form of the story, but take care to separate the grain from the husk." Elsewhere he crystallizes his ideas of what he saw in the Perfect Man as opposed to the man learned in the law:

> The Sufi's book is not a thing of ink and alphabets—
>   'tis nothing but a heart as white as snow.
> The schoolman's provision is the marks made by the pen.
>   What is the Sufi's provision? The traces of his steps
>   [on the Path].

Knowledge (Gnosis), in fact, is to be gained by insight or a particular kind of inspiration, not by book-learning, which can only provide the externality of worldly phenomena. The letters r-o-s-e are simply marks on paper; no rose can be plucked from them. If therefore man desires to rise above mere names and alphabetic symbols, he must surrender his identity, his Self.

But there is a side of the Sufi which is not so ethereal, as Rumi makes clear in the vivid detail supplied in his story of the Sufi who came to a convent where members of his brotherhood were living in poverty. He was riding a donkey and was invited in with great warmth when he dismounted at the gate. Willing hands removed the donkey to the stable, and thence, while the owner's attention was distracted, to the bazaar, where it was sold to defray the cost of some luxuries for supper. This little deception brought joy to the whole brotherhood.

> Enough of this basket-carrying and begging,
>   enough of this endurance and fasting.
> We are human beings too, and we have life.
>   We're in luck tonight; we have a guest.
>
>   .   .   .
>
> They ate the food and began the music;
>   the cloister filled with smoke, the dust rose to the roof—
> The smoke of the cooking, the dust from their dancing,
>   the stirrings of their passion and ecstasy.

106

Now they flung their arms about, pacing their measures,
  now sweeping the dais in their prostrations.
(Rarely does the Sufi find fortune such as that;
  it tells why the Sufi's such a big eater,
Except perhaps the Sufi who of Reality's light
  eats his fill—*he* is free of the shame of begging.)
Having gone through the music from beginning to end,
  the minstrel struck a solemn note.
Reciting, "The ass has gone, the ass has gone,"
  he made the company join in his warmth.

Rumi's *Mathnavi* differs in its composition from others
in the same form by plunging directly into the subject
matter, omitting the normal "Invocations to Allah"
and the sections on "The Prophet's Glories and Virtues,"
on "Praise of the Orthodox Caliphs," and on "The
Reason for Composing the Work." Instead there is a
Prelude in the form of a short poem held in special reverence by the dervishes of the Mevlevi order and recited
in their ritual. More than one attempt has been made to
translate it, the best-known rendering, perhaps, being
that in verse by the nineteenth-century Orientalist E. H.
Palmer, by whom it was called "The Song of the Reed."
The reed, or rather the flute made of a reed, is the
principal solo instrument of the small orchestra to whose
music the ritual dances of the dervishes was conducted,
but almost from man's beginning it was the shepherd's
companion in his solitary vigils, and remains so to the
present day. Into it he breathes his immemorial com-
munings and longings and pours out the desires of his
lonely heart. The Sufis used its music as a means of
rousing themselves into a state of fervor, from which the
dance followed naturally. For them it had a special
significance as the symbol of the gnostic or adept in the
Sufi mysteries, torn from his native place, becoming
burdened with a material body, and longing to be freed

107

in order that he may return. His soul, deprived of sympathy, seeks an ear that will listen to its lament and a mate who understands its woes. It is this longing that is expressed in the reed's song:

(List to the reed, how it makes its complaint,
   telling the story of its sunderings.)
Ever since they cut me from the reedbed,
   the whole world mourns at my lament.
I'd pierce my bosom into holes
   fully to utter the pangs of my yearning.
One who lives far apart from his roots
   looks ever to the day of his reunion.

. . .

My secret is not far from my sad piping,
   but there is no illumination there for eye or ear.
Body is not veiled from spirit, nor spirit from body,
   but not to all is it given to behold the spirit.
This lament of the reed is fire, not air;
   (may he that has not this fire be turned to nothingness!).
It is love's fire that descends into the reed;
   it is love's ferment that descends into the wine.
The reed is friend to all cut off from friendship;
   its strains have rent aside all veils.
Who has beheld poison and antidote like the reed?
   Who has beheld confidant and lover like the reed?
The reed narrates the story of the path steeped in blood,
   it tells the tale of the love of Majnun.
Yet in the nonsentient alone may this sense repose;
   the tongue's sole client is the ear.

. . .

No crudity can comprehend what ripeness is.
   Cut short this talk, and so farewell!

In the body of his work Jalal al-Din laid under contribution for relief and illustration nearly all the well-known anecdotes traditional in Arabic and Persian collections, together with a great many of the allegorical stories and animal fables of the kind which make up *Kalila va Dimna*, cognate with Aesop's Fables. Time and again he warns his hearers not to take them simply as entertainment and not to blame him for their apparent irrelevance, excusing himself on the ground that even the Koran needed illustrative stories, which every Muslim believed, to point the moral of its teachings. He often heightened the attractiveness of his anecdotes by putting them into verse and wittily adapting them to the purposes of his mystical themes. Here is one which illustrates the need for fortitude under the painful discipline of the Sufi life. It recounts the story of a man of Qazvin who paid a visit to the barber to have himself tattooed.

The barber said, "What picture shall I put in, my valiant
    friend?"
He answered, "Put in the picture of a raging lion.
My ascendant sign is Leo, so make a drawing of the Lion.
    Do your best and put in plenty of the blue."
He asked, "Where shall I place the picture on your body?"
    He answered, "Put the drawing of the figure on my shoulder."
When he began to thrust the needle in
    the pain of it upon his shoulder took effect;
The gallant client shouted out, "My dear man,
    you're killing me. What picture are you at?"
The other said, "You ordered me to do a lion."
    He said, "With what member of its body do you start?"
He answered, "It's with the tail part I've begun."
    He said, "Omit the tail, my dearest friend.
The lion's tail and rump clean took my breath away,
    his tailpiece stoppered up my windpipe quite.
O lion-maker, let the lion this time have no tail.
    My heart fails at the hurt done by your prong."
The man of wounds began upon another part,
    relentless, inexorable, merciless.

109

Out loud the patient cried, "What member is it now?"
He said, "This is the ear, my virtuous friend."
"Let him have no ear, doctor," said the other.
"Leave the ear and cut the business short."
The pricking started then upon another part.
The Qazvini once again let out a yell:
"This third piece, what member is it now?"
He said, "Dear friend, this is the lion's belly."
"Then," said he, "let the lion have no belly.
What belly's needful to a drawing full [of ink]?"
The barber stood bewildered, much perplexed,
and long stood gnawing his fingers in his teeth.
At last the "professor" threw the needle down
and said, "Has ought like this occurred to any man on earth?
Who ever saw a lion lacking belly, tail, and head?
Allah himself created no animal like that.
Brother, suffer the pain caused by the sting,
that you may escape the sting of your miscreant flesh.
Unto the man who can escape from being,
sky, sun, and moon bow down in reverence;
Since he within whose body the miscreant flesh has died,
can have the sun and clouds at his command."

The insoluble but everlastingly intriguing problem of the why and wherefore of the universe is the constant preoccupation of the speculative poet, and in different sections of the *Mathnavi* the author approaches it from a variety of angles. Being no more capable of solving it than other speculative souls before or since, he indicates that the question had better not be posed, seeing that the answer is beyond human understanding. All that man can do is to apprehend some aspect of what is involved and let his limited reason provide a meaning to what he finds. Jalal al-Din makes this point in the parable of the elephant exhibited by some Indians in a building from which the light had been shut out.

To view it people in large numbers
   came into the darkened chamber.
Since with their eyes they could not perceive it,
   in the gloom they felt it with their hands.
The hand of one man chanced to touch the trunk.
   He said, "This creature's like a water-spout."
Another's hand alighted on the ear;
   to him the creature seemed just like a fan.
A third one passed his hand along the leg;
   he said, "I think the elephant is columnar."
A fourth man laid his hand upon its back;
   "To me," he said, "the elephant is like a throne."
Thus each man from that organ which he chanced upon
   understood the thing, and heard so everywhere.

        .   .   .

The eye of sight's no more than palm of hand,
   the hand cannot reach out to all of it [the elephant].

The Sufi doctrine of the futility of accumulating worldly goods is the ostensible theme of the fable which comes next, but it also emphasizes the dangers of knowing too much. It is the story, told at some length and with a rather insipid ending, though some of the detail is amusing, of a man who begged the prophet Musa (Moses) to teach him the language of the beasts and the birds. Musa refused, until a divine message came to him to instruct the man in at least part of what he demanded, in order that he might appreciate the dangers and make his own decision: "Place the sword in his hand, remove his disability, that he may become a warrior for the faith—or a highwayman." Musa accordingly taught him to understand the language of the dog outside his door and of the domestic fowls.

At dawn, in order that he might make a trial,
   he stood in expectation on his doorstep.

The maid shook out the tablecloth, whence fell
  a piece of bread, remains of last night's supper.
A cock pounced on it as though it were in pledge to him.
  The dog said, "You're unjust. Begone!
You can eat grains of wheat, but I
  by nature am unable to eat grain.
Wheat, barley, and the other seeds
  you can eat, you lively singer; I cannot.
This scrap of bread is our portion, our only bread;
  you'd snatch this little morsel from the dogs."
The cock spoke up, "Wait; don't be anxious;
  God will grant you something in its stead.
This man's horse is on the point of death,
  tomorrow you'll eat well; abate your fear.
The horse's death will mean a feast for dogs;
  meat you'll have in plenty, untoiled for, and unearned."
On hearing this the owner sold the horse;
  with yellow face the cock came nigh the dog.
But on the morrow too he snatched the bread away—
  that cock did. Then said the dog, reviling him,
"Smooth-spoken cock! What more of such deceits?
  You rob, you lie, and have no spark of light.
Where is the horse you said was like to die?
  A blind astrologer you are, completely void of truth."
The knowing cock this answer gave to him,
  "His horse did perish, but in another place.
He sold the horse and so escaped the loss,
  throwing the loss on other people's backs.
But tomorrow now his mule is sure to die,
  and dogs alone will profit from that gift."
The mean man sold his mule without delay
  and was relieved at once from loss and woe.
Next day the dog addressed the cock and said,
  "Prince of liars, with your drum and tom-tom!"
He said, "He sent his mule for sale in haste;
  his slave boy will be stricken down tomorrow.
When that slave dies, then every kind of food
  will kinsmen shower down on dogs and beggars."

The owner heard—and sold that slave of his,
  escaped from all the loss so that his features glowed.
In gratitude and exultation, "I," cried he,
  "have thrice escaped from damage in short time.
Since I acquired the tongue of birds and dogs
  I've stitched the eyes of evil fortune up."
Next day the starving dog called out,
  "Prevaricating cock, where are your odds and ends?
What more of lies and trickeries have you?
  Nothing but falsehood flies from out your nest."
"Heaven forbid," said he, "that either I or mine
  should ever be afflicted with deceit.
We cocks, like muezzins, speak the truth;
  we watch the sun and see the time is right.

.   .   .

But tomorrow he [the master] is very sure to die,
  his heir, in grief, will sacrifice an ox.
The owner of the house will die, depart;
  tomorrow much good food will come your way.
Pieces of bread, luxuries, and victuals,
  high and low will find along the street;
The slaughtered ox and dainty cakes of bread
  he will lavish, not delaying, on all dogs and beggars."
The horse's death, the mule's, and the slave's
  were fate revolving round this deluded fool.
He fled from loss of wealth and the pain of it,
  increased his wealth, yet spilled his blood.
Why these disciplines for dervishes?
  Wasting of the body means endurance of the soul.

Allusions here and there in the *Mathnavi* are evidence
of the author's having been criticized by his contemporaries
for his failure to provide any precise guidance on the
Sufi Path, and, more seriously, for his inability to demonstrate the difference between the solid and obvious things
which stood before men's eyes, and which to them were
real, and the mystical Reality he was concerned with.

In the sixth book of the work he attempts an answer to these criticisms, wrapped up in the story of a drunken Turkish amir and a minstrel. The jongleur had been singing, in the stock phraseology of the ghazal, about the charms of his beloved, the words of the lyric being:

"Art thou a moon or a doll? I know not what thou wouldst
    desire of me.
I know not what service I may do thee—shall I be silent or
    describe thee in words?
The marvel is that thou art not apart from me; yet I know
    not where I am or where thou art.
When thou dost draw me, I know not whether 'tis to thine
    embrace or to [shed] blood."
Thus he opened his lips in song, making his theme "I know
    not, I know not."

The Turk lost all patience with this. He seized a mace and would have brought it down on the unimaginative singer's head if an officer had not prevented him, telling him it would be wickedness to slay the man in a fit of rage. The amir retorted with refreshing common sense:

"This constant repetition crushes my spirit, and I will crush
    his head.
You wretch, if you don't know, don't talk rubbish; if you do
    know, sing something to the point.
Tell me something that you know, you crazy bore; don't go
    on with 'I don't know' and 'I don't know.'
If I ask you whence you come, you quack, you say, 'Not
    from Balkh, not from Herat.'
If I ask you what you lunched on, you answer, 'Not on wine,
    not on cabob,
Not on dried meat, nor savory bread, nor lentils.'
  Tell me only what you did eat, and no more.
Why at such length chew over things like these?"
  The minstrel answered, "Because my object is a mystery.

114

The positive escapes until all else is negatived.
    I negated that you might catch the scent of affirmation.
In my song I play upon the theme of negating;
    when you die, death will disclose the secret to you."

The passage is almost a parody, perhaps set down in self-criticism, of Jalal al-Din's own agnostic position as it appears in one of the odes in the *Shams-i Tabriz* collection. It has been finely paraphrased by R. A. Nicholson in his *Selected Poems*:

Lo, for I to myself am unknown, now in God's name what must
    I do?
I adore not the Cross nor the Crescent, I am not a Giaour nor
    a Jew.
East nor West, land nor sea is my home, I have kin nor with
    angel nor gnome,
I am wrought nor of fire nor of foam, I am shaped not of dust
    nor of dew.
I was born not in China afar, nor in Saqsin, and not in
    Bulghar;
Not in India, where five rivers are, nor Iraq nor Khurasan I
    grew.
Not in this world nor that world I dwell, not in Paradise,
    neither in Hell;
Not from Eden and Rizvan[1] I fell, not from Adam my lineage
    I drew.

Unlike the *Mathnavi* passage, however, the ode ends on a positive, and to the mystics a satisfactory, note:

In a place beyond uttermost Place, in a tract without shadow
    of trace,
Soul and body transcending, I live in the soul of my Loved
    One anew.

[1] The guardian of Paradise.

SIX : SA'DI AND HAFIZ
OF SHIRAZ

While Jalal al-Din Rumi was in his convent in Asia Minor reflecting upon the mystery of life and on the One-ness of the universe, the poet Sa'di was active in his native Shiraz distilling in verse the mundane experiences accumulated during many years of travel. The Mongol hordes that had annihilated cities, with all their long-established institutions, which in any way impeded their advance into Transoxiana and the northern regions of Iran, encountered no opposition in the southern and south-western regions, where the reigning families hastened forward to offer their submission and payment of tribute. Nevertheless, conditions in Fars were by no means tranquil, and Sa'di was obviously glad to find a patron and live a life of seclusion where he could devote himself to moralizing and poetry.

It was for the most part in Shiraz that he produced not only the *Bustan* (*The Scented Garden*) and the *Gulistan* (*The Rose Garden*), two works which secured him undying fame wherever the Persian language is known, but also a great many ghazals and laudatory qasidas, the former of which deserve far more consideration than they have received from the critics. The *Bustan* forms an excellent introduction to the whole range of Persian didactic mathnavis of mystic-ethical lore, of which a great many exist. Its ten chapters are headed respectively: "Justice, Equity, and Governmental Administration"; "Benevolence"; "Love (Physical and Mystical)"; "Modesty"; "Resignation"; "Contentment"; "Self-restraint"; "Gratitude"; "Penitence"; "Devout Meditations." It by no means follows that the contents of any chapter will be exactly those indicated by the headings, because the artist roams at will over the whole of his experience and sets his inventiveness to work when actualities fail him.

As in the *Gulistan*, expediency is the main lesson taught, although the purely ethical spirit is not lacking, and approval is given to a wide and humane toleration. This is admirably expressed in the story of the prophet Ibrahim and the poor wayfarer, which occurs in the second chapter.

For a whole week of days no wayfarer came
    to be guest at the board of the Friend [of God] Khalil
        [viz., Ibrahim],
Whose practice was never to breakfast at dawn
    until from the road a poor trav'ler came in.
He went forth and on ev'ry side scanned the wastes;
    far off on a bleak torrent-side he espied
A man lone as a willow in that barren place,
    his head and his beard white with the snow of eld.
Warmly he spake words of greeting and comfort,
    and fittingly offered a place at his board:
"O you that are dear as the sight of my eyes,
    with me, of your kindness, come take bread and salt."
With good will the ancient hastened his footsteps,
    aware of the usage of sainted Khalil.

The servitors ready to welcome the guests
    allotted to him a place of high honor.
At command they prepared a bounteous tray,
    about which the guests settled each in his place.
The company uttered the grace, "In God's name,"
    but to Khalil's ear came nought from the beggar.
Thus then he addressed him, "O ancient of days,
    the aged's devotion I see not in thee.
Is it not custom when of food you partake,
    to mention His name who provides for each day?"
Said he, "On my path no practice I follow
    which my Magian elder pointed not forth."
Then 'twas that the well-fated prophet perceived
    that his beggarly guest was nought but a giaour.
With insult he drove him away from the house
    because to the pure the unclean are proscribed.
From Almighty God came an angel voice down,
    with awful reproof calling, "O Ibrahim,
A hundred years I gave him both bread and life,
    to you it was irksome to grant it but once.
Although he bows down to give homage to fire,
    why hold back from him generosity's hand?"

Sa'di is a master in the art of setting down in a few
verbal strokes a scene that comes to life as we read. An
excellent example in the second chapter of the *Bustan*
calls, up the crowded bazaars of a great city, the bustle
and stir at a public spectacle and the brutality of the
shah's Turcoman bodyguard charged with the task of
keeping order:

A youth one day gave a coin to a beggar,
    and therewith the aged man's hunger appeased.
Fate caught him in crime, the soldiery held him;
    the Sultan decreed his death on the gallows.
The gallop of Turks, the mob in a turmoil,
    spectators in doorways, in streets, and on roofs.

The old beggar there in the midst of the crowd
    seeing the youth held in the officer's hands,
Felt his heart stirred to compassion and pity,
    the youth having won him with generous gift.
With loud voice he called out, "The Sultan is dead!
    He's left all the world and borne off his proud soul."
Thus saying he wrung both his hands in despair,
    while the Turks all listened, swords ready to hand.
Confusion befell them at hearing the cry.
    With shattering blows at heads, faces, and backs,
Stumbling in haste to the gates of the palace
    they galloped—and there saw the Shah on his dais.
The youth ran away; the old man was dragged
    by the neck to the foot of the Emperor's throne.
With majesty grim he inquired of the man,
    "What reason possessed you to call for my death?
My spirit is pure, seeking only the right;
    why did you desire me such cruel wrong?"
The gallant old man raised his voice in reply,
    "O thou to whose word the whole world is in thrall,
Through that lying cry that the Sultan was dead
    you died not—and a wretch escaped with his life."

The scene described may well have been suggested
by some incident in Sa'di's own experience, but it is
permissible to the artist to let his imagination roam.
A much-quoted specimen of his skill in the art of fiction
comes in a story laid in India, which country he is hardly
likely to have reached, in spite of vague hints to the
contrary. He recounts the incident as though it had been
an actual occurrence.

In Somnath[1] I saw an ivory idol,
    jewel-decked as Manat[2] was before Islam.
With such sublime skill had the sculptor carved it
    that the mind cannot picture a thing more fair.

[1] In Bombay province. Famous place of pilgrimage, with ruins of
temples and mosques.
[2] An idol worshiped in Arabia in pre-Muhammadan days.

From every clime the caravans traveled
   to behold that body though it lacked a soul.
The princes of China and Turkey all wished—
   like Sa'di—to own that stonehearted idol.
Men of eloquence came from all the world's shores
   to that tongueless image to humble themselves.
I marveled to see how all this could occur;
   wherefore should living men bow to a dead thing?
To a priest with whom I had had some concern,
   a courteous cell mate whom I thought a friend,
"O Brahman," I said in a voice most gentle,
   "In this wondrous place I marvel to see
How men are bewitched by this helpless image,
   and how they lie bound in this pit of error.
Its hand has no strength and its foot cannot move;
   once thrown to the ground it would not rise again.
Don't you see how its eyes are nought but amber?
   Pure folly it is to seek truth from these stones."
At these words my friend turned into a foeman;
   he blazed up in anger and held me tight fast.
He called to the Magians and convent elders,
   a group that for me held not one kindly face.
Those Pazand-reading[1] misbelievers assailed
   me like dogs for the sake of that piece of bone.

          •   •   •

There remained I helpless as a drowning man,
   seeing no resource but only to endure.
When you see a fool is insensate with rage,
   your hope is to yield and to give soft replies.
To the chief Brahman there I gave soothing words,
   saying, "Ancient in Scriptures, Master of Zand,
This idol is pleasing to me as to you.
   Its figure is handsome, its face steals the heart;
its outward seeming fills me with wonderment—
   of its inward meaning I know nought at all.

[1] The poet mistakenly attributes the Magian sacred book the *Zand* and its commentary the *Pazand* to Hinduism or Buddhism.

In this sacred place I am newly arrived;
    'tis rare for a stranger to know good from bad.
Upon this checkerboard you are as the vizier;[1]
    adviser are you to the king of this land.
What truth lies within the shell of this idol,
    of whose votaries first you must reckon me?
To bow as all men do means going astray;
    happy the traveler aware of his road!"
At that the Brahman's face kindled with pleasure.
    He joyously said, "Happy-spirited one,
Your question is right and your act commended.
    He who asks for a guide arrives at his goal.
Like you I have voyaged and traveled afar
    and seen many an idol dead to all sense.
But this which you see here, each morning at dawn
    raises its arms to the great god of justice.
If you desire it, remain here this night,
    at dawn the rare sight will be vouchsafed to you."
That night I stayed there as the elder desired,
    like Bizhan held captive in dungeon of woe.
The night was as long as the Day of Judgment,
    about me the priests stood unwashed at their prayers.

       .   .   .

Then sudden a drum beat a thund'rous tattoo
    and a priest crowed out like an untimely cock.
That black-vestmented Preacher, the pitch-dark Night,
    from its scabbard unsheathed the bright sword of Day;
The fires of morning flared up into a blaze,
    in a flash the whole of the world was alight.
Misguided Magians, their faces unlaved,
    appeared in each doorway, each square, and each street;
In the city no man or woman remained,
    in the temple no room for a needle was left.
I was filled with distress and drowsy with sleep,
    when lo, the dumb image held both arms aloft!

[1] In the Persian game of chess the "vizier" or "counselor" takes the place of the European "queen."

A roar brust forth loud from the crowd gathered there,
  as though the wild ocean were stirred into rage.
When the temple once more was free of the mob,
  the Brahman towards me turned round with a smile.
Said he, "I am sure you no longer have doubts;
  the truth is quite patent and falsehood has fled."
Beholding him thus in his folly held fast,
  delusion and fancy sunk deep within him,
Nothing more dared I say approaching the truth,
  for truth must be hidden from men sunk in lies.

        .   .   .

Pardon I begged of that ivory object
  on its gold-plated throne and platform of teak.
A kiss I bestowed on the wretched thing's hand
  (Accursed be it and its worshipers too!);
For several days I worshiped as they did,
  becoming a Brahman and reading the Zand.
When in the convent I found myself trusted,
  I scarcely could hold myself down on the ground.
One night most securely I made fast the door,
  then ran like a scorpion to left and to right.
The platform I scanned both below and above
  and spied there a curtain embroidered with gold,
Behind it a fire-tending vestmented priest,
  a shrine devotee, with a cord in his hand.
At once it was patently clear to my mind—
  as iron in David's hand softened to wax—
Without any doubt when he tugged at the cord,
  the idol would raise both hands in devotion.
Abashed stood the Brahman at seeing me thus;
  disclosure brought shame on all happenings there.
He fled, but I followed close on his heels
  and headlong I threw him down into a well.

As fiction the story requires to be elaborated very little
further, but having put it forward as something in which
he was personally concerned, Sa'di ends by excusing

himself for what would certainly be regarded as a crime by saying it was a question of the priest's life or his own.

At various times the "complete" works of Sa'di have been published, revealing him to be an author with numerous sides to his genius. Many hundreds of qasidas, both in Persian and in Arabic, are ascribed to him and he is regarded by his fellow countrymen as a master of the ghazal, a worthy forerunner of Hafiz, who is considered supreme in that genre. The qasidas were of the usual type composed to celebrate the glories of patrons or of notables who had distinguished themselves to the extent of having befriended Sa'di, but many were elegies or odes of mourning.

It is the ghazals, rather, which call for remark. The majority are of the normal type, with love—whether physical or mystic—as their motive. But a great many were also composed under the stimulus of friendship, a fruitful subject for poetry not only in Persia but also in Europe, more especially in England in the seventeenth and eighteenth centuries, although fallen rather out of fashion since. The many hundreds containing Sa'di's pen name were gathered some years after his death into a number of divans. In them the poems are arranged in no order but that of the letters of the alphabet as they occur in the rhymes, making it impossible to trace how the poet's ideas and skill developed or to determine which were the products of immaturity and which came in periods of riper thought. If one is looking in them for references to passing events, it becomes a matter of hazardous guesswork, but this applies to the divans of all the poets.

What the ghazals betray is the fact that Sa'di's heart and mind were constantly pulling in different directions, the religion in which he was brought up and the fatalism of his environment being at cross purposes with his life experiences. Even the Sufi mysticism which was his refuge from the problems of existence was not completely satisfying, because beyond it he saw the humanly inexplicable way in which Fortune threw its favors about —lavishly to the worthless and grudgingly to the deserving.

In all Sa'di's divans the striking features of the ghazals are the lyrical quality of the language and the rhythm within the construction. One might very well go to them, as Pope said, "As some to church repair, Not for the doctrine, but the music there." Rhythm, cadence, and turn of phrase, unfortunately, cannot be transferred into a foreign tongue without distortion or serious weakening of the force of the original text. As for that, words may sometimes be put in by the author merely for the sake of the jingle and may consist of sentiment appropriate enough to the place and time of composition but unacceptable to modern taste as artificial and insincere rubbish. The only resort of the translator is to do the best he can with prose renderings of what he considers characteristic. Here, to begin with, is a conspectus of Sa'di's views on his problems and those of humanity in general:

Sufi, bewildered in the fetters of good repute,
> if you do not drink down to the dregs, you will never escape
>> your woes.
What gain or loss accrues to the Kingdom of Eternity,
> whether you know the Koran by heart or are an idol-
>> worshiper?
Of what [further] advantage to you is piety, if you dwell in a
> palace?
How can misbelief harm you, if you are blessed by fortune?
Both saint and sinner are powerless to command prosperity;
> learned and unlettered are failures in their search after truth.
You that are a victim held in a trap, your struggles will not
> free you;
>> you fowl caught fast in a snare, your fluttering is of no avail.

.   .   .

Set no hopes upon the things of this world, Sa'di,
   as it has dealt with others so it will deal with you; so
      abandon hope and go!
If you have wit and sense and an understanding mind,
   I'll speak to you as man to man; otherwise you are less
      than the beasts.

Distress at the thought that he may be sailing under
false colors is clearly expressed in the following ode:

I live within the cloister a dissembler full of pretense,
   garbed in patched dervish robe, an impostor, void of inner
      truth,
Worshiper, in the temple of fraud and trickery, of an idol
   equal to Manat and Suva', Lat and 'Uzza.[1]
Without shame I boast of my manhood,
   having set my soul to wickedness like any minstrel girl.
Under this old cloak I am the Pharaoh[2] of the age for
      hypocrisy,
   proclaiming myself Musa [Moses] himself in his agony on
      Sinai.
I entered the idols' temple and saw its devotees;
   but, of them all, the worshiper most confirmed am I.
Like me, like me, Sa'di, drink deep of the clear wine and the
      lees,
   for it is when I have drunk wine that the Master holds me
      most dear.

An ode that appears to be amongst Sa'di's youthful
exercises in the art of ghazal-writing is this:

You have come tardily, my dear one, languishing,
   not soon will your cloak depart from my hand.
Upon the fire of my love for you the water of contrivance
   though lavishly poured will have little effect,

---

[1] Idols worshiped in pre-Muhammadan Arabia.
[2] The Koran says he made a pretense of conversion to the true faith.

From the sight of you, there can be no turning away,
    there can be no closing of a door in your face.
Compared with your noble stature,
    the garden cypress is a humble thing.
Unhappy he that lives from you apart, at ease is the body in
        union with you.
With each amorous glance your eyes cause blood to flow;
    but when does the drunken slayer grieve for his chance
        victim?

Sa'di, out of the snares of the beauteous,
    as long as life lasts you will never escape.
And if you will not lay your head upon that threshold,
    what will you do? What other door exists?

Sa'di is said to have lived to an age remarkable for his
time, some biographers putting it at a hundred and ten
lunar years, equivalent to a hundred and six solar years,
and giving the date of his death as either 1290 or a year
later. Fame had come to him during his lifetime, but he
seems to have become pathetically conscious of the decline
of his powers of literary creativeness long before the end,
if his words can be taken as expressing genuine feeling.

The time is here when weakness comes and strength departs,
    from the speech of the sweet singer power departs.
Before the breath of autumn nears and while the clearness
        lingers in the waters,
    the sweet perfume will have departed from this rose tree.
My feet no more will have the power to walk;
    well for him who has taken heed and trodden virtue's path.
Until the day when the water in the brook flows backward,
    Allah knows, my stream of tears will ever descend.
My aim has been that, like sandalwood, in the fires of reflection
    I might consume myself and let the scent pervade the world.
Sa'di's sole capital has been his sweet speech.
    This of his will remain. What will depart I do not know.

An unidentified Persian critic once pronounced the opinion that:

For verse three prophets there be
—though "there is no prophet after me" [Muhammad said]—
For descriptions, qasida, and ghazal—
They are Firdausi, Anvari, and Saʿdi.

It is fairly obvious that the jingle was composed at some date, probably in the early fourteenth century, before the appearance of Shams al-Din Muhammad, "Khwaja" Hafiz, of Shiraz, who today is acknowledged the master of the erotic ghazal. It was he who inspired Goethe to compose his *West-östlicher Divan*, the German poet characterizing him as a great happy genius and lovable guide to life who rejoiced in showing his fellow men how to avoid inessentials, encouraging them to live for the best they had and to enjoy it. "Out of his poems," said Goethe, "streams a constant liveliness suitably modulated. Within their framework men are contented, happy, and clever, taking their share of the world's goods, looking on from afar at the mysteries of God but also keeping aloof both from the practice of religion and from sensual desires, for this kind of poetry must maintain a skeptical balance."

Much of the work of Hafiz was composed in the city of Shiraz, whose pleasant haunts, especially the garden of Ruknabad and the *Musalla*, the prayer-place beyond the walls, refreshed by cooling breezes, he celebrated in a number of his odes. From allusions here and there in the divan it has been deduced that he was born there at some date in the ten-year period between 1317 and 1326. He died there in 1390, having been absent for only a very short period of his lifetime. Compared with the ravages they had inflicted on the northern territories of Iran, the

Mongols had been sparing in the province of Fars, of which Shiraz was the capital, but local princely rivalries and two invasions by the dreaded Tamerlane had not left it tranquil. Yet Hafiz enjoyed a tolerably comfortable existence under the auspices of his first patron, Prince Abu Ishaq Inju, who reigned for about ten years from 1343 and was then deposed. For long Hafiz was also the friend of another local ruler, Shah Shuja', frequently mentioned in the ghazals.

Like other poets who were obliged to return thanks for favors received, or to prepare the way agreeably for favors expected, Hafiz wrote panegyrics on those princes, viziers, and noblemen who had befriended him. It is a Persian legend that Hafiz was never mercenary enough to compose adulatory verse. What lies behind the legend is the fact that his panegyrics were not written in the qasida form but in that of the ghazal, in whose Sufi garb he clothed the usual lavish compliments.

Modern, and especially Western, scholars dissatisfied with the inadequacy and fancifulness of the materials supplied by the Persian biographers have been led to search the divan for allusions which might throw light on events and persons figuring in the poet's life. It is known that his patron, Abu Ishaq Inju, an easygoing person of not very strong character, met his death on the scaffold, and that another of his benefactors, the Shah Shuja' already mentioned, had to banish the poet from Shiraz at the insistence of the religious authorities, who disapproved of his irregular life and the encouragement he gave in his verse to dissolute practices and unorthodox opinions. This period of exile from his beloved city and of separation from his friends produced most of the ghazals in which Hafiz bemoans his lot and implores his old patron to take compassion on his misery.

Whether Hafiz was genuinely a Sufi it is difficult to decide in view of the very mixed character of his ghazals and of the interpretations that can be placed upon his words. The Oriental commentators, almost to a man, took his verses, however sensuously worded, in a purely mystical sense. Yet a standard biographer of Sufis, namely the fifteenth-century author Jami, although he characterizes Saʿdi as one of the most accomplished of Sufis, hardly recognizes Hafiz as being one at all, on the grounds that it was uncertain whether he had an acknowledged "pir," or spiritual guide, or whether he belonged to a dervish order. However, Jami calls him "Tongue of the Unperceivable" and "Interpreter of Secrets" and says his language is so impregnated with mystical ideas that the adepts are not unanimous over the question whether he was a Sufi.

The hesitation is understandable in view of the contrasts presented by different parts of the divan. What, for instance, but a spiritual meaning can be attached to the allegorical ode next cited (which, in translation, is bound to lack the weight, texture, and color, that is to say, the music and rhythm, of the original words):

In eternity long ago the rays of Thy beauty breathed of the
      passing of darkness;
  love was unveiled and set the universe ablaze.
Thy countenance created glory; the Angel beheld it, but,
      having naught of love,
  became through envy the essence of fire and set Man
      aflame.
From this flame Reason aspired to kindle a lamp;
  envy's lightning flashed forth and destroyed the world.
The Impostor wished to enter the stage upon which secrets
      are divulged;
  the hand of the Unperceivable came and struck that
      uninitiated one to the heart.

Others when casting dice have struck fortune;
   my grief-stricken heart it was that cast for more grief.
The higher life lusted for the dimple in your chin,
   and seized those tresses writhing curl on curl.
And Hafiz wrote his joyous ode of love for you
   when the pen proscribed all good to the gladsome heart.

The pantheistic teaching propagated by Hafiz that any road may lead to God could hardly have been reconciled with the creed that Muhammad, as the Apostle of Allah, was the only guide to salvation. Clearly therefore no true believer, whether learned in the Muslim code or not, could attach anything but an allegorical significance to such an ode as that beginning:

In the tavern of the Magians I see the light of God.
   Behold the marvel of the light and where I see it!
Who is he that drinks deep in this tavern, O Lord, the door
      of which
   I see in the point to which men turn in supplication and
      direct their prayers?
Boast not of your glory, O King of the pilgrim train, for you
   look to the house, whereas I look to the owner.

Even less than that ode can the free-thinking verses distributed throughout the divan have been to the taste of the leaders of Islam. An outstanding example occurs in the ghazal which begins:

None has seen your face and there are a thousand rivals for you;
   you are still in the bud [veiled] and a hundred nightingales
      [sing] for you.

It continues:

Where love is, no difference lies 'twixt convent and tavern;
   wherever it exists, the glory of the Beloved's face appears.
Where men worship at service in the [Muslim] cloister,
   there also is the monastery bell and the Name [inscribed]
      on the Cross.

The break in the two parts of the ghazal is only apparent, for it must be repeated that the poet arranges his
verses, in the Persian idiom, as he would thread pearls
on a string, each verse being almost always self-sufficient
in rhythm and sense. This accounts not only for the
difference in the order of the lines observable in different
copies of the same ghazal but the seeming variety of
subjects contained in it. A criticism of this multiplicity
of themes is put into the mouth of Shah Shuja', who is
reported to have remarked that he could see no continuous
thread running throughout any one ode, but that three
or four lines would be devoted to wine, a couple to Sufi
lore, and one or two to some talk of the beloved. Hafiz,
presumably out of discretion, is reported to have agreed
to the justice of this comment. The fact is, however, that
the lines generally reflect different facets of the same
subject, or they are variations on a theme.

Hafiz encourages the mystical interpretation placed
on his verse by saying: "My object, whether in the mosque
or the tavern, is union with you; that I have no other
thought but this, God is my witness." For the most part,
however, his attitude to life is that of the realist, and he is
ironical at the expense of people who affect to regard
ordinary human needs as nonexistent or, worse, as sinful.

Those who by a glance turn earth into a philosopher's stone,
    can they have the corner of an eye to spare for me?
Far better conceal my pain from fraudulent physicians,
    for they may find its cure in the pharmacy of the Unseen.
Since well-being lies neither in being dissolute nor ascetic,
    'twere better for men to leave all to the grace of God.
The Beloved does not lift the veil from off his [her?] face;
    why then has each a tale full of description to unfold?

The poet concludes:

Drink wine, for a hundred sins veiled away from other men
    are better than flaunted piety and plain hypocrisy.

Such an attack as this on pretense and flaunted religion is said by some modern commentators to have been excited by the fanaticism of Shah Shuja''s successor Mujahid al-Din, to whom the law was something that had to be obeyed, generally by others rather than by himself. These commentators hold that any mention of the *Muhtasib,* or censor, in the divan refers to that tyrant, who on the pretense of enforcing religion, suppressed the accustomed and innocent pleasures of the people. A typical passage is:

The Censor is now a holy doctor and has forgotten his sins;
    it is the legend of *me* that lingers in the marketplace.

. . .

I had a dervish cloak that covered more than a hundred faults;
    that patched robe was pawned for wine and music and only a
        [Christian] girdle remained.

Ironies like these are not the ground upon which affection for Hafiz based itself in the hearts of his countrymen. The political allusions are long forgotten, in much the same way as those which made *Gulliver's Travels,* and some say even English nursery rhymes, pungent in their day. It is the music and the charm of the verses that have remained, though the ghazals may differ in character, from youthful studio exercises—full of the rose and the nightingale and the thorns which those who would pluck the rose must suffer—to poems of maturity in which some of the bitterness of life is allowed to peep through. Here is part of one containing a spark of true emotion and a thrill of personal experience that may provoke a response:

'Tis a mysterious subtle thing that stirs up love;
    its name is neither ruby lip nor golden down.
Not in eye, tress, cheek, or mole lies loveliness,
    but a thousand subtleties work to captivate the heart.

132

In a more intimate mood comes this:

Long ago, far more than now, were lovers' thoughts alive in
      you;
  your kindliness towards me won renown in every clime.
Long ago, when this green roof and azure sky were being
      raised above,
  my beloved's eyebrow formed an archway to the vision of
      my eye.
From the dawn of past eternity to the end of everlasting night
  our fond love rested on one firm pact and one covenant.

.   .   .

Blame not me, if on the Night when fates were written we
      drank together;
  my beloved came in merry mood—and by the archway stood
      a cup.
If then, the rosary's thread was parted, hold me guiltless;
  my arm was about the Saki of the silver thighs.
The songs of Hafiz were composed in Adam's day, in Paradise,
  to the book of Roses sweet came the adornment of his leaves.

Perhaps to Persian taste the best, and in its position the
most apposite, of the poet's ghazals is that which has
been inscribed on his tomb at Shiraz. It may be rendered:

Where is the glad news of our union, that I may rise above life?
  I am the Bird of Resurrection and can rise above this
      earthly snare.
By my love for you, were you to account me your slave,
  I should rise beyond lordship of all existence.
(Lord, from the cloud of Thy guidance send down rain,
  before I rise and vanish like dust from off the earth.)
Beside my tomb with wine and music seat yourself,
  that sensing your fragrance I may rise from within the grave.
Arise, O figure sweetly moving, let me behold your stateliness,
  that casting life and world aside I too may rise.

I am old, but let the night come when you draw me to your
      breast,
  that at dawn I may rise from your embrace with youth
      renewed.
On my dying day, a breath's delay grant me, that I may
      behold you,
  so that like Hafiz I may arise leaving life and world behind.

SEVEN: NASIR KHUSRAU

A significant figure in Persian literary history, but one who has for centuries aroused controversy and debate amongst the pundits, is Nasir son of Khusrau, or "Nāṣir-i Khusrau" in the Persian idiom. Being a poet as well as a philosopher and the author of a well-written book of travel, he is not easy to place in any one category. As for personal details about him, he says in one of the qasidas in his divan that he was born in the year 394 of the Hegira (1003–1004), probably at Qubadiyan in the province of Merv, once part of Khurasan but at the present day included in Soviet Turkmenistan. At the time of his birth the Ghaznavid dynasty were still in nominal control of the country, but they were overthrown by the Seljuq Turks about thirty years later, both these warrior families owing allegiance to the Sunni (orthodox) form of Islam.

Nasir appears to have had the schooling that permitted him to become an official of the government—in the revenue department at Merv—where he claims to have acquired distinction among his colleagues. There he remained until his forty-second year, when, for no reason that he gives, he was transferred from Merv to Juzjanan in the Balkh district. This seems to have been a less important post, and he confesses that he took to drink and drank steadily for a whole month. He tells us in his travel diary that at the end of that month he had a dream in which a figure appeared to him and asked him how long he proposed to continue his addiction to wine, which deprived man of his wits. He replied that the scientists had invented no other means for tempering the woes of existence in this world. But to that the retort came: "Loss of self and sense is no palliative. None can be called wise who declares that oblivion is the hint for mankind to follow. Rather seek for something that will heighten your wisdom and sensitivity." When Nasir asked where he was to procure it, the figure oracularly said, "Seekers are finders," and pointed a finger in the direction of Mecca.

When Nasir awoke, he remembered his dream and admonished himself, saying that now that he was awakened from his last night's sleep he must rouse himself from his slumber of the past forty years. He reflected that to find peace he must change his whole course of life, and accordingly he resigned his post and set out on his pilgrimage, which was to last seven years. The narrative of his journey is full of details of the places he passed through or visited, the people he met, and the hardships and adventures he underwent on his way. One thing he never mentions is how he, presumably not a person of substance or rank in the worldly sense, was received by men of importance at various stages of his journey and found the means to return to Balkh across hundreds of miles of difficult and dangerous territory. A plausible explanation is that while he was in Cairo, where an Ismaili Fatimid caliph was enthroned, he was converted,

seemingly from "Twelver" Shiism (which teaches that
twelve Imams constituted the legitimate headship of Islam)
to Ismailism, one of whose tenets is that there are only seven
Imams, of whom Ismail was the last. The Ismaili sect
was strong in northeastern Persia, but was regarded as
heretical elsewhere, so that its adherents kept their
identity secret and formed "cells" in various parts of the
country. From one to another of these Nasir was presumably passed on.

The cloud of mystery which shrouds this author is
briefly indicated by Daulatshah, the biographer of poets,
who remarks, "Some say he professed the unity of God
and was a pious ascetic; others accuse him of being a
Natural Philosopher and a Materialist, as well as of being
a believer in the transmigration of souls." That he
worshiped at a mosque and outwardly displayed signs
of adherence to some recognized school of Islamic religious thought is obvious from the circumstances of his
age and environment. From the *Safar-nama* (*Travel
Diary*) it might be inferred that he was a Sunni, but that
work has without doubt been censored, and perhaps
altered, in the Sunni interest. From the fact that he has
for long been known, in Persia at least, as Nāṣir-i Khusrau
"Alawi," it may with some confidence be deduced that
he was of the Shia persuasion, even if his divan did not
provide abundant evidence of his scorn for the orthodox
"schools" of Islam. One instance may be cited from a
qasida which has an additional interest as supplementing his account of what induced him to undertake his
travels:

Forty-two times the skies in their orbit had passed over me
   and my persuasive spirit besought me for knowledge.
The laws of the heavens and of the recurrence of days and
        nativities
  I had learned from sages and read in books.

Yet since I had found my own body sounder than other men's
   I said that surely in Creation there must be someone better—
Such as the falcon is amongst fowls and the camel among beasts,
   as the date palm is among trees and the ruby among jewels,
As the Koran among books and the Ka'ba among buildings,
   as the heart among bodily organs and the Sun among the
      stars.
Pondering thus my heart was distressed with thought,
   the philosophic spirit probed into thought's results.
From Shafiite and Malikite and the words of Hanifa,
   from the world's Elect I sought a trusty guide.
But when I asked Why and Wherefore and for a sure sign,
   they writhed in impotence; the one became blind, the other
      deaf.

       ·   ·   ·

So I arose from my home and went upon my journeyings,
   caring nought for household, garden, or familiar sights.
From Persian and Arab, from Hindu and Turk,
   from Sindi, Greek, and Hebrew alike,
From philosopher, Manichee, Sabaean, and Free-thinker I
      begged
   for what I needed and endlessly sought.

       ·   ·   ·

Questioning I went from this city to that one,
   inquiring I voyaged over this ocean to that land.
They told me, "The basis of the Law rests not on reason,
   for it was by the sword that Islam was established."
But I would not blindly follow (nor hid my argument),
   for not through blind conformity is God revealed.
When God desires to open mercy's door,
   difficulty is made easy, all roughness smoothed away.
One day I reached the gates of a city to which
   the heavenly bodies were enslaved, the horizons all
      submissive.
A city whose gardens all were filled with fruits and filled with
      flowers,
   its walls all adorned and its earth tree-covered.

The lands beyond were resplendent as brocade,
  its waters honey purified, like Kauthar [in Paradise].

  .   .   .

When I arrived there a wise man said,
  "Here find what you seek, and go no further."

This delectable city is by inference to be identified with
Cairo, at the time of Nasir's arrival the seat of the Fatimid
caliph Mustansir, who was also for a time the overlord of
Mecca. It was here, probably, that Nasir was converted
to Ismailism and furnished with means and documents
which would enable him to return to Khurasan and there
carry on propaganda for his sect, although, as has been
said, no word of this appears in his travel diary. Soon
after his return, the date of which is given as October,
1052, he was made to leave the capital and reside in
Yumgan, a district situated in the region of the Upper
Oxus River. There he lived for many years, dying at a
date unspecified, although his tomb is still pointed out in
the place.

In spite of, or perhaps because of, the rigors of life and
the loneliness which a man of his attainments must have
suffered in those remote and harsh surroundings, he
devoted himself to setting down his thoughts in prose and
verse, producing more than one of his philosophical
treatises and a large number of qasidas. Most of these
contain a reference to injustices inflicted on him by the
Khurasanis, to the dreariness of his life, and to the penalties
of old age. Thus he says:

Surely through the act of these madmen I am here imprisoned
      at Yumgan.
Thou knowest all secrets, and to Thee, O Lord, I cry for aid
      against Thyself.

The implied criticism of Allah's inexorable settling
of man's destiny is echoed more than once in Nasir's

divan, and one whole qasida displays at some length his skeptical attitude, even accusing Allah of being inconsistent and capable of being placed in a dilemma. In the course of it he exclaims:

If a peasant sows barley, he will not harvest wheat from it:
Thou didst determine the fate of all things on the first day of
        past eternity,
  but the requital will only be seen at eternity's end.
Thou didst bring Creation to pass in order to be obeyed;
  why, therefore, was it needful to create Satan?
I could utter much, but have not the effrontery;
  scarce can I draw breath through fear.
Not a hair's point of belief do I possess
  to let me hear the doctrine of a brainless pietist;
But the teachings of the learned sage should be received,
  since it is from the oyster that pearls must be obtained.

. . .

I know not how matters will stand at the Resurrection,
  when there comes the summing up of my reckoning.
If I urge my cause I am afraid
  Thou mayst display Thy wrath, from which I could not
    flee.
Hadst Thou desired me to refrain from this questioning,
  Thou shouldst have made me a beast of the field.

If, at the Last Assembly, I debate with Thee,
  Thou must drag my tongue from out my mouth.
If thou dost not then remove my tongue from me,
  I shall not be impotent in argument;
And if Thou dost remove my tongue, 'twould be a wrong,
  and why then have created Justice in any guise?
But bid them bear me off to Hell;
  what use is all this give and take?
Yet it befits not justice and benevolence,
  to harm another when the fault's one's own.

Next world's ways will not be those of this;
  none will there see things advanced by force and bribery.
Upon Thee lies the onus of decision in all things;
  and canst Thou have recourse to anyone but us?
Thy slave can be accused of no offense;
  Thou didst Thyself bestow the power to choose.
Thou didst leave the flaw in human hearts
  through which the Devil may enact his schemes.
Thou didst accord to love acquaintanceship with lust,
  that by sating passion man may attain to bliss.

In that cynical vein the poet continues for many verses
more. According to a distinguished modern Persian
critic, S. H. Taqizadeh, this qasida is not in tune with the
remaining poems in the divan and is therefore in all
probability not the work of Nasir. But the question of
what distinguishes the true from the spurious Nasir
inevitably presents itself. The riddle is made all the harder
by the legends which early sprang up about his magical
powers and his contacts with the realm of the supernatural. These figure prominently in the pseudo-
autobiography which is found prefixed to some editions
of the divan and is itself an excellent piece of prose writing.
A small portion is worthy of being quoted, if only to
provide an insight into the kind of education traditionally
received by a man of letters. It reads:

From the beginning of my life I was passionately eager to acquire
the sciences and all the accomplishments. By the time I was
nine years old I had achieved the honor of learning by heart
the Divine Book and knowing the mystery of the Revelations
which had been sent down from Heaven to the Prophet—upon
whom and whose kin be Allah's blessing! For the next five
years I was occupied with language and grammar, prosody and
rhyme, and for the three years after that I studied the science
of the stars and astronomy, geomancy, Euclid, and the Almagest.
From the age of seventeen and for fifteen years thereafter my

time was spent in learning the Law, the Traditions of the Prophet, the abrogating and abrogated verses of the Koran, and various other subjects. [Here follows an extended list of the scholarly works he read.]

By the time I had reached the age of forty-four years I had acquired the arts of subduing supernatural beings to my will, of constructing talismans, and of practicing magic, and all things connected with these arts. . . . In the passage of time it occurred to my mind that there should be no secret in the world left undisclosed to me. It happened, through the vicissitudes of chance, that I came to Egypt, where I was appointed to be the king's vizier and so occupied a lofty position and had a great retinue attached to me. . . . As time passed the scholars and savants there began to look with jealousy on my influential office, and one day in my absence accused me to the king of being a heretic and a dualist. They wrote a decree by which I was condemned to death and my book of Law to be destroyed by fire. Their false words induced the king to take immediate action, and an attack would have been made on my life if one of his sons had not given me timely warning. Forsaking all my offices, my dignities, and my splendid retinue, at dead of night I regretfully departed from Egypt, taking my younger brother Abu Sa'id with me.

The narrative takes the pair to Baghdad, where, it says, Nasir spent a period in the service of Caliph Qadir. But as the caliph of that name died A.D. 934 and the real Nasir was not born until 1003, there is clearly something amiss here. However that may be, the story goes on to tell us that our hero was then sent on a mission to the Qarmatian heretic ruler of Gilan, one of the South Caspian provinces, whose guest—apparently an unwilling one—he remained for a considerable length of time. At last his brother demanded of him why, with his knowledge of the supernatural, he did not have recourse to it and so escape. The proposal appealed to him and he applied for leave to hand over his office to his brother so that he himself could set out on a propaganda mission to spread the heretic king's doctrines.

Nasir used the respite given him to invoke the spirits who were to help him escape. One of them told Nasir that if he gave the command he was prepared to destroy the king immediately. He replied, however, that he was unwilling to incur any suspicion of having been instrumental in causing the king's death and that it was better to strike him with a progressively worsening disease that would make him relax his control and enable him (Nasir) to achieve his object. In due time the king fell ill, and Nasir, as chief physician of the realm, was summoned, but gave an evasive answer when asked to diagnose the trouble. The sickness took its expected course until the king was on the point of death, when once again Nasir was summoned. The story goes on:

I went before him in dread because it is a grave matter to cause a man's destruction. As I approached, he said, "Son of Khusrau, I am aware that it is you who are killing me by suborning the spirits to bring my career to an end. Still, since I have had a regard for you and your wisdom in the past, I now permit you to depart from this country unharmed."

In fear and trembling [at the king's knowledge] I returned home and told my brother that we must leave the city that very night, and, summoning one of the spirits, I commanded him to stop the king's tongue. This he did, and meanwhile I devised a plan by which my brother and I could escape from the city. I went to the king's son and told him that his father's disease was curable, but only by means of a particular herb which grew outside the city, in the desert. I was permitted to go and, with my brother, departed . . . reaching Nishapur after many hardships.

The story is then told of an adventure which befell Nasir in that city. He had stopped at a cobbler's in the bazaar to have his shoe mended, when suddenly a great clamor was heard coming from the outside. Promptly the cobbler dropped what he was doing and rushed off to discover the cause of the disturbance. He was away for some time and returned carrying a piece of flesh on the end of his awl. To satisfy Nasir's curiosity he explained that the notorious heretic Nasir Khusrau had been seen in the city, where his poetry had been recited, that he had been seized and cut to pieces by the mob. The flesh on the end of the awl was his (the cobbler's) share, given him as reward for the part he had played in the proceedings. Nasir hastily departed, saying that he could not delay for a moment in a city where heretical verses were recited.

We are told in this piece of fiction how its pretended author spent the later part of his life. When coming to Yumgan he had made himself known to its chief, who offered him the post of minister, but Nasir excused himself on the ground that being now advanced in years he was no longer fitted to undertake worldly office. His real reason, however, was that he was afraid of the hostility of the local religious leaders. He retired to a cave, set up a number of magic talismans for his protection, and for twenty-five years remained there practicing pious exercises and learning to discipline his bodily appetites, to such good purpose that he ate only one meal each thirty days. Thus he found peace after he had for long suffered the oppression of kings, the hostility of the learned, and the intolerance of the religious lawyers.

At last the days of my life reached one hundred and forty years. My physical strength had suffered a serious decline and my mental powers lost their keenness. It was then that a heavenly Voice informed me that the end of my life was approaching. . . . [To my brother I said,] "When the spirit departs tell no one, but wash my body yourself and dig a grave for me in the rock in the true center of this cave. While you are busy in the task, two of the best instructed amongst the Jinn will present themselves before you and request to give you assistance. Do not refuse them, in any manner whatsoever. . . . When you have buried me, burn my book on Greek science and the one which deals with magic and invention . . . . and yourself depart from the village after I am gone.

The narrative is completed by Sa'id, who says that, acting in accordance with his brother's behest, he constructed a great talisman outside the cave and over it broke a bottle of unknown contents which Nasir had consigned to him. Instantly the entrance to the cave became indistinguishable from the rest of the mountainside in which it was situated, all trace of it vanishing.

This fanciful invention differs greatly in substance from the sober narrative provided in Nasir's account of his travels. Nasir gives precise details of all the places of note that he reached, so that naturally there are long statements, based on accurate observation, about the sacred buildings and other well-known features of Mecca, Jerusalem, Cairo, and other great cities. More interesting perhaps for our purposes are the personal touches and the casual references to the everyday life of the author. He tells how, having finally decided to leave Mecca after the last of his pilgrimages, he hired a camel and after several days' journey across the desert came to a district called Matar. There, he says, was no one ruler or governor, but groups of thieves and murderers, each with its own chief and constantly at war with the rest.

Some distance beyond Matar there was a place which boasted four strong forts in the space of half a parasang. It was the home of the man from whom he had hired his camel, and there he had to remain for fifteen days because there was no available escort to conduct him safely through the next stage of his journey. Each tribe had its grazing ground, which it regarded as its own preserve, and no stranger was allowed to pass through without paying toll, failing which he was liable to be stripped naked. In this case the escort proved to be the chief of the next tribe along Nasir's route and so was able to ensure the traveler a safe passage. In one part of the desert he encountered men who in the whole course of their lives had never drunk anything but camel's milk and thought that the whole world did the same. Others regularly ate lizards. But Nasir confesses he could neither drink camel's milk nor eat lizard's flesh.

The hazards of Nasir's undertaking are illustrated by his account of what happened to him at Falaj, some stages nearer home. Like most of the *Safar-nama* this episode bears the marks of authenticity where the text has not been cut. It tells how the inhabitants there, who lived by robbery and violence, were not only desperately poor but completely uneducated, so that when he tried to sell some of his books to satisfy his daily needs there was no one to buy. During part of the four months he was compelled to remain there, he occupied some idle hours in covering a wall with calligraphic writing. With this evidence of his skill the men of Falaj were so impressed that they offered him a hundred maunds of dates if he would decorate the *mihrab*—the niche in their mosque facing in the direction of Mecca. In their eyes this represented a gift of considerable value, and in fact it enabled him to keep body and soul together for a large part of his stay.

The diary ends in prosaic fashion with statistics of the distances covered on the journey from Balkh to Cairo via Mecca and the return home through Basra and the province of Fars. The author claims that all his statements are true insofar as they describe what he himself saw, and he craves the reader's forgiveness for anything reported at secondhand which should prove to be disputable.

EIGHT : PERSIAN
SATIRISTS

It has been seen that poets at the courts of the Iranian princes who had won their independence of the caliphate were encouraged by hopes of reward to exercise their talents by lauding their patrons or pouring scorn on the rivals of those whose favor they wooed. For third parties, unless they were connoisseurs in the art of qasida writing, most verses composed with such motives have had little appeal. The Western reader has failed almost entirely to be interested, looking to content rather than to form in his reading and rejecting the idea of being able to buy praise or blame in the open market. The Persian, even though understanding something of the technique involved, has turned from satires as containing language apt to offend the accepted canons of good taste or personal allusions so obscure as to be meaningless.

There were, however, exceptions. A satire, even if it was directed at some individual unknown, might contain some amusing verbal quip or a touch of malice which brought a smile. The fact that the Arabic and Persian word for "satire" connotes vilification and personal abuse explains why Persian anthologists and literary biographers, when choosing representative passages from the authors they are dealing with, nearly always ignore what they regard as unworthy aspects of their genius. Nevertheless Firdausi himself, one of the giants of Persian literature, included in his *Shahnama* some bitter invective against Shah Mahmud of Ghazna, who rewarded him for his labors with a penny a line instead of the gold coin he deserved. The poet said:

> Had Mahmud not been of so mean a spirit,
> He'd have raised me on high to position and rank.
> And learning's a thing that is foreign to him
> Or else he'd have set me aloft on a throne.
> Of his ancestors none was possessed of a crown
> And therefore he knew not how monarchs behave.

Quatrains with their anonymity provided excellent cover for satirists and many a scurrilous jibe has been introduced into the divans of poets, probably without their knowledge. Here is one of unknown parentage which is aimed at the author's countrymen in general. Each line has a supplementary one rhyming independently.

> The Feast has come all things to gladness to restore—as a
> bride just wed.
> Into his cruse the Saki ruby wine will pour—as a cock's eye,
> red.
> The bridle of prayer and the muzzle of fasting—for another
> year
> The Feast from off the heads of these asses will lower—a
> prospect to dread.

ANVARI

One of the recognized masters of the qasida, whether laudatory or denigrating, was the twelfth-century Anvari,

who was court poet to the Seljuq sultan, Sanjar of
Khurasan. Towards the end of his life he declared that
he had repented of the way in which he had misused his
powers, and says in the course of one of his odes:

Yesterday a rhymester asked me if 'twas ghazals I composed.
    I said I had washed my hands both of satire and of puff.
"Why?" he asked. I answered, "That business was sheer folly;
    the cause once past never more from the void returns.
Lyrics, eulogies, and squibs, I wrote all three
    through greed or rage, to which you may add lust.
The lover's full of torment all night long, thinking
    how to describe lips sweet as sugar or the curling of a lock.
The flatterer's day is spent in painful pondering
    where, how, and from whom he can earn five pence.
The critic's like a weary dog consoled with the thought
    that he can seize a victim feebler than himself.
Shall I then compose lyric, puff, or satire? Lord forbid!
    Too far I've tried my spirit; too deeply outraged mind."

Two shorter compositions of Anvari's are worth repeating.
One is a lampoon on a trio of government officials:

Majd al-Mulk's wisdom in ruling the realm
Is bad as verdicts by Judge Nasihi.
Who, Lord, is his like for futility?
Wait, I know. It is Taj-i Salihi.

The second is on a wealthy, corpulent friend:

Don't despise me when you see me afoot;
Against walking I never have complained.
The movements of the heavens are all free;
They are not held in stables, kept in flocks.
Because you ride, you need not proudly boast;
You've no cause for bragging ostentation.
You're like a mountain, and where that's concerned
Only earthquakes can stir it up to move.

'UBAID ZAKANI

Contemporary with Hafiz of Shiraz about the middle of
the fourteenth century, and having the same patron in
Sheik Abu Ishaq Inju, was 'Ubaid Zakani. He devoted
a good many of his laudatory qasidas to this patron, who
appears not to have disbursed what was expected of him,
for the poet is always complaining about the fewness of
his assets and the multiplicity of his debts. Most Persian
literary historians ignore his serious work as a critic of the
evils of his time and regard him, because of the bawdy
stories he told, as a reprehensible character, with the
consequence that manuscripts and printed editions of his
verses and his prose compositions are rare, and where
found are expurgated. His countrymen's estimate of him
is betrayed by a fanciful portrait prefixed to the Tehran
edition of 1955, which shows him as a little man squatting
on the ground with his hands modestly crossed and
with a disarming, if rather dissipated, cast of countenance. His sallies at the expense of the good and respectable
can never have been much to the taste of persons in
authority.

In addition to a divan consisting of eulogistic qasidas,
of ghazals and quatrains, 'Ubaid's surviving works consist
of several compositions in prose and one or two short
mathnavis. These are packed with a mixture of irony,
wit, and ribaldry, frequently untranslatable—even if the
words were contained in the dictionaries—casting a
somewhat lurid light on social conditions in Iran in the
days when they were being described. Actual specimens
may present some idea of the general tone. The first
comes from his *Ethics of the Nobility*, a prose work made up
of essays on the standard virtues together with the same
virtues as reinterpreted by the men of his time. It forms
part of the chapter on Justice.

The Abrogated Principle. The great men of the past regarded justice as one of the four great virtues and upon it based the structure of this world and the next. It was their creed that "Heaven and earth stand upon justice," and they considered themselves bidden by divine command to uphold it. Sultans, princes, nobles, and viziers held it to be their chief duty to propagate justice, and to maintain the well-being of their subjects both civilian and military, recognizing that upon such practice rested their power and good name. . . .

The Preferred Principle. Our contemporaries hold that this code of behavior is the worst possible and that ruin follows inevitably on justice. This they have clearly proved, on the ground that the whole fabric of empire, government, and economics depends on stern control. Unless a man is feared his orders will not be obeyed; [without that] all men would have the same status, the entity of the realm would be destroyed, and good order would be disrupted. Nobody would stand in awe of a man who executed justice (which Heaven forfend!) or refused to flog, or kill, or practice extortion, or who failed to drink himself into a stupor and make great displays of temper and rage against those under his authority. In such circumstances, kings would not be obeyed by their subjects, children and slaves would pay no heed to what their parents or masters said, and the whole well-being of the state and those who served it would fall into ruin.

People say, "Equity bequeathes adversity." What clearer evidence of that is there than this, that as long as Persian kings like Zahhak the Arab and Yazdigard the Sinful (who now honor the first positions in Hell) . . . practiced evil, their empire flourished and their rule prospered. When, however, the time of Chosroes of the Happy Spirit arrived, he, in the feebleness of judgment and foresight attributable to himself and his addle-pated ministers, chose the path of justice. Within a short time the pinnacles of his palace toppled to the ground, the sacred fires at which they worshiped were at one blow extinguished, and all trace of them was expunged from the face of the earth.

* * *

Chingiz Khan, who today in despite of his rivals occupies the deepest compartment in Hell as the model and chief of all Mongols early and late, did not secure the rulership of the whole earth until he had destroyed myriads of victims with his merciless sword.

Anecdote. It is set down in Mongol history that, when Baghdad was stormed, Hulagu Khan commanded that any persons who had escaped the sword should assemble before him. He questioned each class about its circumstances and, after acquiring full information, he said that artisans, being indispensable, were to be dismissed and go back to their work and that merchants were to be provided with capital to trade on his behalf. Concerning the Jews he said that since they were an oppressed people he would be satisfied with the poll tax from them. Effeminates he sent to his own harem quarters. As for qadis, learned elders, Sufis, Hajjis [those who had performed the Mecca pilgrimage], preachers, men who claimed descent from the Prophet, beggars and religious mendicants, wrestlers, poets and storytellers, them he set aside with the remark, "These are superfluous in the scheme of Creation and wrongfully consume God's bounty," and had them all drowned in the river, so that the earth was disencumbered of their vileness.

Thereafter, inevitably, the sovereignty became firmly established in his family's hands for nearly ninety years, their prosperity increasing with every year that passed. But then arrived the miserable [Sultan] Abu Sa'id, who got into his head the mawkish idea of Justice that led him to earn the title of "the Just." Within a very short time his reign was brought to an end, and the princes of the line of Hulagu Khan and all their high endeavors vanished because of the ambition of Abu Sa'id. . . . Blessings on those great and successful men who led mankind out of the dark misguidedness of Justice into the light of proper direction.

Of 'Ubaid's short mathnavis, one which achieved fairly widespread repute is the "Tale of the Cat and the Mouse." Probably because of its political implications, which perennially had their significance in Iran, it was from time to time revised or rewritten. It tells the story of how once upon a time in the city of Kirman there lived a veritable dragon of a cat. Its belly was a drum, its chest a breastplate; it had the tail of a lion and claws that a leopard might have been proud of.

One day the cat went into a tavern in chase of the mice that played between the wine jars, behind one of which he lay in wait. Suddenly out of a hole a little mouse jumped up onto one of the jars, put its head in, and took a long drink. Then, filled with valor, it shouted out, "Where's the cat, for me to tear its head off and fill its hide with straw? Cats are mere dogs to me when we stand up to each other in battle."

The cat heard this but said nothing, only sharpened his claws and teeth. Suddenly he sprang and got the mouse in his claws, where the miserable wretch pleaded with him. "I am your humble slave," it said. "Forgive me if I have sinned. I was drunk, and if I said improper things—drunkards often do."

"Stop your lying," said the cat, "I'll hear no more falsehoods." And with that he killed the mouse and ate it up. But then he went remorsefully to the mosque, performed the prescribed ritual washing of his hands and face, wiped over his feet and said his prayers piously as a mulla. Then he did penance for his misdeed, saying with tears, "O Creator, for the innocent blood that I have shed I will bestow two maunds of bread in charity."

A mouselet listening behind the pulpit swiftly carried the good tidings to the other mice. "The cat has turned religious. He has become a self-denying believer and a true Musulman." Rapture broke out amongst the mice when they heard this story and in sheer affection for the cat began to prepare gifts of wine, roast lamb, cheese, dates, pilaw, and other delicacies, which seven of their chiefs carried in state and placed before him with their ceremonious respects and good wishes.

The sight of the mice filled the cat with thoughts that now at last he was going to make up for the long periods of abstinence

he had suffered in the past "for the sake of the Merciful One."
With a bound he was amongst them, seizing four in his claws
and one in his mouth. The rest escaped to carry the tragic
news back to their friends.

"Pour ashes on your heads!" they exclaimed. "The cat has
torn to pieces five of our chieftains." After conferring together
they donned mourning garb and sent a deputation to the capital
to present a statement to their king about the outrage which the
cat had inflicted upon them.

"In the past," they complained, "he took only one of us in a
year. Now that he has become a penitent and a Muslim he
takes us five at a time."

The story ends, rather abruptly, leaving its readers, with
proper discretion, to draw their own moral from it.

Throughout the period of stern government that came
with the Safavi shahs, when obedience to royal command
and to the dictatorial behests of the religious authorities
left no room for independent judgment or public criticism,
satire would have been indulged in only at great personal
risk. There was no possibility even of concealing dis-
cordant opinions in the language of the Sufi poets, because they were regarded as little better than infidels
with their laxness of religious observance and their
latitudinarian views about the demands of the laws of
Islam. Furthermore, satire was often merely panegyric
in reverse, and panegyrists of living patrons were discouraged by monarchs who held that the only objects
of glorification were the holy imams, descended through
the national hero Ali from the Prophet's daughter
Fatima.

The ban upon free speech remained for long after the
Safavids had been driven from the throne, until the habit
of criticism had become atrophied. But in the nineteenth
century European ideas began to infiltrate into Persia,
and travel abroad had given men of education and

experience in affairs an insight into what was lacking in their own country. A movement began for social justice and a popular constitution that would limit the powers of despotic rulers and give the people in general a voice in the government of their own country. The Qajar shahs, who were reigning at the beginning of the twentieth century, had little desire to yield to demands such as these. But their despotic and irresponsible rule, together with the relentless pressure exerted on Iran by foreign powers, of whom Russia and England were regarded as the most burdensome, wrung expressions of discontent from patriots who had become aware of the possibility of reforms.

All the best writing of the period had these lofty aims in view. By its very nature it demanded, in order to have the desired effect on its public, a pen dipped in gall and vinegar. Only that could rouse Persians, long steeped in indifference to public affairs, out of their apathy. Oppressive foreign powers had to be scarified, despotic rulers and reactionary landlords had to be lashed or held up to scorn, until they condescended to do their duty towards the mass of the people who suffered their injustices. But as in other countries living under arbitrary rule the author who gave rein to his emotions and preached a dangerous liberalism was liable to have his works suppressed and his person cast into jail. For a long period, therefore, the voices raised in criticism came from expatriates, whose writings had to be printed abroad and smuggled into Persia in order to reach their public. Their compensation was that they were read with far greater earnestness than their Western colleagues, because they satisfied the needs of men risking their lives in some underground movement, who sought from the written word not pleasure and diversion but stimulation and guidance in planning their activities.

ZAIN AL-ABIDIN OF MARAGHA

Ephemeral publications were the easiest means of spreading revolutionary ideas, but occasionally books were written to lay bare the wrongs under which the people suffered. One which was said to have had very considerable effectiveness was *The Travel Diary of Ibrahim Beg*, by Zain al-Abidin of Maragha. Ostensibly fictional so far as the names of the characters were concerned, it may well have been a record of actual experiences. It describes how the hero, Ibrahim Beg, born in Egypt but of Persian origin and nationality, having for long visualized the land of his fathers as an earthly Paradise at last finds an opportunity of visiting it and seeing the reality for himself.

The story is told in deadly earnest, lashing out in every direction at the government and its officials, at the venality of the judges, and the corruption to be found amongst all the people, from highest to lowest, who performed any service to the general public. Typical of many scenes portrayed is one in a Turkish bath (hammam), where a number of men are gathered and shown lying about at their ease. As the hero enters he observes that their beards, mustaches, hands, and feet are stained with henna. The story continues:

By the side of the cold plunge I saw two men dyed in this fashion, with hubble-bubbles in their mouths. I asked one of them if he belonged to the town and he answered that he did. I then asked him for what purpose the people there stained their hands and feet with henna. With a look of astonishment at me he said, "First it's the proper thing to do, and second it softens the hands and feet."

I heaved a cold sigh from the very depths of my sore heart and said, "My dear sir, find a salve that will soften your hearts equally. How long will you continue merely ruminating over your country's progress and about safeguarding its rights?"

156

Strong feeling overcame me. I called for the attendant and from somewhere heard an answering cry of "Coming!" In a little while I saw a ghostly figure standing over me; when I had arrived at the baths I had not been able to see anything clearly because the steam was so thick. I said, "Bring me some soap. I'll wash myself. But you shall have your tip."

NINE : THE MODERN ERA

The poets so far dealt with are only the highest peaks in the great ranges of Persian poetry. In the catalogues of many important libraries scattered throughout the world, large sections are devoted to the divans of thousands of Persian poets and to biographies of them. In mass their output is prodigious, contributions to it having been made not only by Persians but also by natives of the old Indian subcontinent and of Turkey, where knowledge of the Persian language was, and in part remains, as much an essential of an educated man's equipment as knowledge of French in eighteenth-century Europe. A list of the names of versifiers would have little point, for the vast majority are only dimly familiar even to scholarly Persians.

JAMI OF HERAT

Yet there is one poet, Jami of Herat, who remains to be mentioned as having worked in the classical tradition of Sa'di, Nizami, and Hafiz. He did not achieve the standards set by his predecessors, but the extent and variety of his compositions made an impression on his fellow countrymen, whose opinions were followed in the West to the extent that several of his works were translated into European languages. He was a member of the Naqsh-bandi order of dervishes, but did not therefore think it necessary to cut himself off from society, and he was in fact closely attached to the court of the Timurid ruler of Herat, whose vizier, 'Ali Shir Nawa'i, himself a poet, was Jami's intimate friend.

A "quintet" on the model of Nizami's *Five Treasures*—ultimately enlarged into a "septet"—is his chief work, but other aspects of his versatility are to be seen in his *Baharistan* (*The Abode of Spring*), his biographical dictionary of Sufis entitled *Nafahat al-Uns* (*Zephyrs of Tranquillity*), and his three divans. The subjects dealt with in the *Baharistan* differ from those of the *Gulistan* and lack Sa'di's worldly and good-tempered outlook on life, but there is not lacking a characteristic touch of bawdy to appeal to the groundlings. The evidence that he was a much more convinced Sufi than his model comes in the biographical dictionary, and that he was less inspired as a poet is clear from the three divans, arranged to include the verses belonging respectively to his youth, middle age, and declining years.

The strong mystical strain in Jami and his Sufi con-nections led him to employ the obscure verbiage of his kind, allied to elaborate metaphors, flowery language, and an exaggerated accumulation of epithets. Defects of this nature, indulged in to excess in both verse and prose, became common with writers in the period following Jami, until their work became the butt of parody and ridicule. Here is a comparatively mild specimen of this baroque style of writing. It is taken from a rendering, more or less literal, of the introductory paragraph of the seventh of the eight "Gardens"—that dealing with poetry and poets—comprised in Jami's *Baharistan*.

The Story of the rhyme-balancing Birds of the Grove of Eloquence and of the ghazal-singing Parrakeets of the Sugarcane Brake of verse-making.

According to the science of the early philosophers, poetry is speech composed of phantasy-inducing ingredients; that is to say, it is of such nature that into the imagination of the hearer it injects ideas which will bring about the acceptance of something, or its rejection, whether that something be in itself true or not and whether the hearer believes it to be true or not. For instance, [poets] say, "Wine is liquid rubies or flowing jacinths," or, "Honey is a bitter or salt substance exuded by bees." The later philosophers considered that meter and rhyme must form part of the definition.

This involved floweriness must not be taken as typical of Jami's work in general, but it vitiated much of Persian writing, especially in India, in the three centuries after him.

THE SAFAVI DYNASTY

Jami had lived under the protection of a Timurid prince at Herat, capital of one of the rival provinces into which Persia had broken after the death of Timur (Tamerlane). The country remained in a state of disruption until a conqueror appeared on the scene who was able to impose unity on the land. He was one Ismail, descended from a Sufi saint who claimed authority on the score of being a member of the family of 'Ali, the first imam and fourth caliph. This Sufi saint had been the pir, or spiritual director, of an important order of dervishes which drew its membership not only from Persia but also from Turkish tribes in Asia Minor, and from his name Safi al-Din the dynasty which Ismail founded was called "Safavi."

Ismail himself had been left an orphan at the age of three by his father's death in battle, but he was brought up by loyal supporters and at the age of thirteen, being even at that age a person of strong character and physique, he left his home in northern Persia and made his way to Azarbaijan, gathering adherents as he went until he had seven thousand men backing his cause. With this force he captured Tabriz, the capital of the province, where in 1501 he proclaimed himself shah, and, as a direct descendant from 'Ali, commanded that henceforth the religion of his subjects throughout Persia was to be that of the Shia. This "party" of 'Ali held strongly the principle of hereditary rulership, in opposition to that of free election by which the Arabs had, nominally, chosen the caliph.

The new ruler turned out to be harsh and bigoted, but he had the merit of standing up to the aggression of Salim the Grim, sultan of Turkey, with whom he was in rivalry for the mastership of the whole of Islam. His courage and determination kept Persia its independence and special religious character, which it has retained ever since. In the intervals of combating their enemies both outside and inside the country, his descendants busied themselves with religious activities, but at the same time they encouraged such artistic pursuits as architecture and miniature-painting, so that some of the best extant examples of these arts date from their era. Nevertheless Safavi interest in religious observance and theology and in the propagation of Shia doctrine led to the discouragement of Sufism with its easy-going attitude towards matters of faith and religious practice and particularly towards the restrictions imposed by the doctors of religion. Consequently, although great volumes of theology were produced in abundance, the humanities suffered. Poetry was especially affected because much of it had been impregnated with Sufi lore and language, and for the two

161

centuries of Safavi domination no poet, essayist, or composer of literary works of general interest has any claim to special mention.

QA'ANI

The line of the classical tradition was indeed broken for nearly four centuries, until the beginning of the nineteenth century. It was then that the dynasty of the Qajar shahs came to the throne, after the disturbed period which followed the traditional internecine quarrels and the inevitable Safavid collapse before the Afghans in 1722. During those three hundred years there were no doubt petty rhymesters and imitators of the great models of the past, but no great poet of the caliber of a Sa'di, Hafiz, or even Jami appeared on the Persian scene, even though religious poetry received considerable impetus from the prevailing zeal of the Safavids and their successors. During that interval, however, the Muslim courts of India became a haven for Persian poets, mystics, and theologians; and India, a second home for Persian litera-ture, produced a large number of poets, many of them distinguished for the subtlety of their thought and imagery. In Persia the relative stagnation of poetry lasted until about the middle of the eighteenth century, when a group of poets, mainly from Isfahan, pioneered a return to the more vigorous styles of the classical poets. The renaissance of Persian poetry reached its climax with Qa'ani.

Qa'ani was born at Shiraz in 1808, of a father who was himself a poet, and after a period of travel about the country was chosen to be poet laureate to the sovereign, Muhammad Shah, remaining in his office under that king's son and successor, Nasir al-Din, who reigned for almost as long as Queen Victoria in England and recorded his visit to her in his diaries. To judge from the general tone and content of his verses, Qa'ani was very much the heir of the older panegyrists, whose pen could be bought to propagate favorable opinions about anyone who would pay for the service, or to scorn the rivals of any lavish patrons. Yet he also had a remarkable power of composing verses in new modes with rousing life and swing in their rhythm, even though they collapse into a rubble of words when the framework of meter and rhyme is removed.

BAHAR

Of very different caliber was the later poet Bahar, known by the title of *Malik al-Shu'ara* (king of poets). Born in 1880 at Mashhad, one of Iran's places of sacred pilgrimage, he spent his working life as a writer in the composition of verse and prose that would further his democratic ideals. Much of it was contributed to periodical pudlications, his verse being as a rule in line with the classical tradition, although he was something of an innovator and introduced new forms imitated from European models. Much of the subject matter was intensely emotional treatment of events affecting his country and fellow patriots, and he bitterly attacked any outsiders whom he regarded as interfering with the affairs of Persia. Although for a short time he consented to employ his talents in the public service to the extent of acting as Minister of Education, he was critical of the authorities and was more than once thrown into prison for his searing comments on weaknesses in the body politic, the corruption prevailing amongst the ruling class and their officials, and the inefficiency of local government. Yet on the accession of Shah Riza Pehlevi he wrote qasidas of welcome phrased in tactful language.

Almost all his work is frankly didactic, some of it intended to rouse the poorer of his countrymen from their apathy and some to induce the wealthier and more powerful sections of the nation to obliterate the wrongs they had made the rest suffer. Here is a fable (the original in verse) in a gentle mood rare with him:

THE STREAMLET AND THE ROCK

A streamlet broke out of the mountainside
  and on his way encountered a rock.
Gently he said to the stubborn stone,
  "Of your kindness, blessed one, let me pass."
The heavy rock, dark-hearted, thick-headed,
  struck him a blow and said, "Be off, young sir,
I move not even for a stream in full spate.
  Who are you that I should leave my place for you?"
The streamlet, by the stony answer undismayed,
  halted, began to dig and firmly press.
It dug and delved and strove until
  past the boulder it had made a way.
By effort you can reach to any goal,
  attain to any object you may aim at.

Almost until the beginning of the First World War the Persian man of letters preserved the tradition, if not the instinct, that he must express himself in verse rather than in prose, although it was the exception rather than the rule when he was concerned with philosophy, theology, the sciences, or history. Even there an author could use verse for the body of his discourse, and, if he used prose, he was frequently tempted to break what he regarded as the tedium of long stretches of unrhythmical language by inserting at significant points citations from his own or other people's verse, whether in Persian or Arabic.

The tradition of composing in verse, much of it in the old forms, has by no means died out. Here only a few of the older twentieth-century writers can be mentioned, amongst them Dakhaw, Arif Qazvini, Iraj Mirza, Rashid-i

Yasimi, deriving from every class of the community. All had prose works to their credit as well as verse.

IRAJ MIRZA

Iraj Mirza, a member of the Qajar family who was born in 1874 and died in 1926, may be mentioned as advocate of a greater measure of social justice for women in Persia and their release from some of the restrictions and disabilities from which they suffered. Especially did he press their right to cast away the veil, as for example in a poem entitled "The Book of the Veil," which seems to have had a fairly large public. His style, direct and devoid of subtlety, betrays the earnestness of his period.

> Lord, how long will these men remain asleep?
>   The women, how long shall they be enclosed in the veil?
> Is woman not counted human amongst us?
>   Has she no mind to distinguish good and ill?
>
>   .   .   .
>
> When woman desires communion with Thee,
>   no veil hinders, no face band prevents.
>
>   .   .   .
>
> Go, man! Give some thought to living!
>   You are no ass. Give up this asininity!

Persian prose works have a wider appeal than poetry to the European palate, largely because their themes are more universal. Here again there are writers that are worthy of mention, their list growing ever longer with the spread of education and the enlargement of the reading public. Amongst those who have distinguished themselves in the past few decades two are outstanding—Sadeq Hedayat and Muhammad Ali Jamalzadeh. Both are products of Persian birth and upbringing combined with later European education and environment, and they are for that reason not fully representative of the Iranian tradition as it developed amongst its heirs normally resident in their own country and participating in its ordinary life. Their significance lies in having introduced fertile new ideas into that tradition and loosened some of its links with the past.

SADEQ HEDAYAT

Hedayat was born in 1903 into an upper-class family, but seems to have received an unconventional and irregular education. Comparatively early in life he left home and settled in France, where he spent the rest of his life, to which he himself put an end in 1951. His numerous productions, mostly in the form of sketches and short stories, were obviously composed in circumstances of great mental stress and under the influence of what he experienced and read while in France. In all of them are apparent his Kafka-like preoccupation with solitude, misery, and death, especially death self-inflicted. Apart from himself, the characters who appear in his stories were the ordinary men and women he remembered from his childhood days, when he had seen or met them in the streets of Tehran and its outskirts. But his scenes are not all laid in the capital, some being in the provinces, as for example Shiraz, "city of red roses, nightingales, and wine."

Almost everywhere in the stories marked sympathy is shown for the generally subordinate position of the women of Persia, and when his heroine is in conflict with a man it is she who triumphs in the end—a symbol of Hedayat's revolt against tradition. That not much of the joy which normally balances the sorrows of existence appears in these tales, or in those of others of the same school of writing, may be due to deliberate intention, as though with the purpose of making their readers react in protest at their conditions of life. Hedayat's own gloom, however, no doubt stemmed from his personal makeup. His melancholy is exemplified in the following short passage from one of his stories named "The Blind Owl," which in general conveys the atmosphere of Edgar Allan Poe, Dickens, and Zola at their most macabre.

Repose was forbidden to me. How could I rest? I formed the habit of taking a walk every day, close on the hour of dusk. I don't know why it was that I had the urgent desire to find some stream, a cypress tree, and a cluster of water lilies. In the same manner that I had got accustomed to opium, so I had got into the habit of taking this walk, as though some external force compelled me to it. The whole way I was filled with thoughts of her, with the memory of the first time I had caught sight of her. I longed to find the place where I had seen her on that day of festival. If only I could find it! If I could only sit under that tree, peace would be born anew in my life. But alas! There was nothing but sweepings, hot ashes, old ribs, and a dog sniffing about the refuse. There was nothing else. Had I ever in reality met her? Never! All that had happened was that I had caught a glimpse of her by stealth through a crack; through a miserable window in my cupboard of a room. My condition was that of a hungry dog sniffing about and searching among the garbage, running off in a panic and hiding as soon as he hears the men cart the rubbish, and then returning to look for his savory gobbets again. But now the window was shut. For me she was a bunch of fresh, sweet flowers which someone had thrown on the dust-heap.

JAMALZADEH

By contrast with Hedayat, Muhammad Ali Jamalzadeh secures his effects by good humor and a gently mocking style. He was born a few years before 1900, at Isfahan, where his father was at the time a preacher at a mosque and known for his outspokenness. This frankness brought his father into conflict with Zill al-Sultan, the Qajar governor of the province, and compelled his departure for Tehran. There the boy received his early education, being later sent to school at Beirut in Syria and afterward to France. Soon after the outbreak of the First World War he went to Berlin, where, until 1931, he was employed at the Persian Legation, afterward joining the International Labor Organization as his country's representative, a post he still holds.

Although Jamalzadeh's work shows the impact of European, and especially French, literature, his great and growing popularity amongst the educated middle class in Persia is evidence that the innovations he helped to introduce into their own literature are to their taste. His great achievement was the complete break with tradition which he contrived with the publication at Berlin in 1922 of a collection of short stories titled *Yeki būd yeki na-būd* (When something was and something was not), which is roughly equivalent to "Once upon a time." The first story in the collection poked fun on one hand at the ponderous Arabisms of the learned and on the other at the ostentatious use by the intelligentsia newly arrived from Europe of foreign terms and expressions incomprehensible to the man in the street. In compensation, Jamalzadeh crammed his stories with "common" people speaking their everyday language in their own way. To those whose reading was confined to books written in the customary style this tongue newly imported into literature was as incomprehensible as Arabic, French, and English were to the masses, and the book had to be provided with a vocabulary of colloquialisms translated into literary Persian.

In a preface that has since come to be regarded as a manifesto and a guide at a parting of the ways, Jamalzadeh set out his doctrine that the time had come for Persian authors to shake off the trammels of their inherited literary forms. Something fresh and unfamiliar was required as a means of educating a public which was too greatly occupied in earning a living to have time for the ordinary formal processes of getting instruction. This new instrument of education he found in the novel, short or long. Here, he proclaimed, was the means by which the people of Iran could be taught something of the manners and customs of the rest of the world and one half of the land shown how the other half lives. With him, as with his compatriot authors, the mainspring of activity was the urge to reform and improve the conditions of life in Iran, a motive that is strongly brought out in his ironical story entitled "The Politician."

You ask how it was I entered politics and came to be a public figure. Four years ago, as you may remember, I was a cotton carder; the job being to remove the seeds from cotton pods. Some days I earned two riyals, some days ten, and for supper I might carry home a couple of okes of bread and a few ounces of meat of some kind. But my silly wife was always nagging at me. She kept saying, "Come on, stir yourself. You stick at your cotton-cleaning and come home every night with your beard and hair covered with cobwebs. Now there's our neighbor Haji Ali. A year ago he hadn't a penny. He does some quiet business, scrapes acquaintance here and there, and now he's getting on in the world. His wife tells me that one of these days he is going to be a member of Parliament, with a hundred tumans a month sound cash, and everybody respecting him. As for you, you'll go on beating cotton till you have a foot in the grave. I wish your hat had a few brains inside it."

Well, as it turned out, she was right. Haji Ali, with nothing else than the coat on his back, had been running round like a dog, and, putting this and that together, there he was, a somebody. His name began to be mentioned in the newspapers—they called him a democrat—and suddenly without a word he was a member of Parliament. There he was, being polite with the Shah and ministers. The fact is, I'm sick of this job of mine; it's the worst of the whole lot. I hate the sound of that cotton-beating; it's worse than the questions they'll put to me when I'm put in the grave. . . .

One night, when my fool of a wife began to nag worse than ever, I made up my mind I'd give up the carding job and take up the same line as Haji Ali. As it happened, my luck was in and God himself helped me to get where I wanted. I don't know how it all started, but someone in the bazaar began shouting: "Close the shops! Let's go to the Parliament!"

I was in my shop, thinking of nothing at all, like a tired donkey. But I was up in a flash, had got the door closed and was out in the bazaar shouting for justice and yelling out things with no rhyme or reason at all. I had heard that it was what people shouted when this kind of thing happened, so I shouted with the rest, just as though I was having a row with my wife at home. Then what a show there was! I said to the crowd:

"Persians! You men who have any feeling for Persia! We are losing our country! How long are we going to suffer? Unity! Concord! Brotherhood! Come on, let us have done with all this! Let us die martyrs and leave a glorious name behind, or else let us live free of this shameful misery! Come on! Up the cause! Show your courage!"

Well, all the tradesmen locked up their shops and the bazaar, but without much sign of interest or enthusiasm. It was just as though sunset had come early and the shops were gradually being shut, the people buying things to take home to supper. All the same the unexpected closing of the shops had its effect, that and the shouts of the apprentices going to the cafes, hoping the workshops would stay closed for several days and give them the chance for a holiday.

As for me, the truth of the whole thing was very puzzling. Could all this be the result of my shouting and yelling? It was like a tea urn with the flame blazing, flaring up with a roar and the whole thing boiling over with a rush. Now I began working myself up until I was a regular ball of fire, using language that surprised even myself, especially when I heard myself say that if the Shah didn't come to our help, we'd drag him from the throne . . . .

Friends argued with me, but I didn't listen and I kept on shouting till the bazaar roof reechoed, drowning the calls of the ice-cream men and the cucumber-sellers. The out-of-work, the blind, and the loungers began to crowd round me, and suddenly I was the leader of an army, like Kaveh the Blacksmith, the man that my son Hasani had learned about at school and told me about at home afterward. I set out for Parliament like a mad camel, with the crowd behind me growing bigger all the way.

.   .   .

The next day everyone was talking about me. I heard men say in the bazaar how with their own eyes they had seen me offered a thousand gold pieces and I had not troubled to look at it . . . . Some months later I was returned to Parliament with the Democratic Party.

EPILOGUE

In this small book, whose purpose has been to guide the reader about the landmarks of Persian literature, attention has been concentrated on the authors whose mother tongue was Persian and whose life was spent in their native Iran. It is such poets, romancers, and essayists who best represent the literary side of Iranian civilization. But Iran at various periods of its long history has far overrun its physical and political boundaries, generally leaving behind a fertile alluvium of linguistic and cultural elements. Thus in the rich lands of Turkistan beyond the Oxus, in Asia Minor and Ottoman Turkey and in the Indian subcontinent—centuries before its partition into India and Pakistan—Persian literature, art, and cultural ideas have been studied and perpetuated. Today the literary language of Soviet Tajikistan is classical Persian, although the written word may be clothed in the Cyrillic alphabet; in the Indian subcontinent, the philosopher-poet Sir Muhammad Iqbal, one of the spiritual founders of the State of Pakistan, gave voice to some of his most profound thoughts through the medium of Persian verse.

Persian has in fact had a continuous history running back for many centuries in the great subcontinent. Princes there for long made it their practice to invite poets, historians, and artists from Iran to adorn their courts, but there was also a native literature produced in

Persian by poets and historians who could rival in genius those of Iran itself. The most distinguished and prolific of them—he is credited with having composed 400,000 lines of verse—was Amir Khusrau of Delhi, who died in 1325. He came of mixed parentage, his father having been of Central Asian antecedents and his mother a Hindu, yet his education and environment led him to express himself best in Persian, while the themes of his romantic mathnavis were for the most part those that had been used before him by Nizami.

Amir Khusrau was only one amongst many in Hindustan who turned to Persian for a medium of literary composition, for the "corpus" of Persian verse and prose which has grown up there in the course of the centuries is a very large one. Indo-Persian literature has in fact become an independent genre, in much the same way that American literature, although using English as its medium, has grown away from the parent body and become differentiated from it because of the fresh circumstances which gave it birth. Another parallel to the variant character of the Iranian Persian and Indo-Persian literatures has been found in the differences between the Persian and Mogul art forms.

Persian, however, was not merely a tongue acquired and used by poets and historians. They formed only a small percentage even of the educated. It was also the language of diplomacy, of the law courts in the Muslim states and provinces, and of polite intercourse in the upper strata of the people. Its prevalence in quite early times is apparent from the Urdu form of Hindustani, which is a mixture of the Persian brought by the Mogul conquerors and the Sanskritic dialect spoken by the people they conquered.

Persian cultural ideas have spread far into China and Southeast Asia, and traces of Persian occupation have been found on the east coast of Africa. A map, therefore, showing the area in which Iran has left its mark would, in addition to the outposts mentioned, cover the western half of Asia including Asia Minor to the west and a great part of the Turcoman Republics of Soviet Central Asia. For long periods in the past Iran's cultural leaders were concerned with the spiritual aspects of man's earthly existence and his ultimate destiny, questions with which the riddle of good and evil was intimately bound up. In recent times, in Iran as elsewhere, more immediate goals for human reasoning powers have obtruded themselves, the problem of man's existence requiring urgent consideration. Demands for higher standards of living are associated with a thirst for knowledge, which is being met in Persia by strenuous efforts to spread education. This is being done by various means, including the re-editing and publication in new forms of the standard Persian classics, the translation of famous works written in foreign languages, and the furtherance of archeological studies. The more modern side of education, with its emphasis on science, is at the same time being fostered, but has by no means dulled the universal taste for poetry and *belles lettres*, which are being produced as abundantly and read, or listened to, as eagerly as ever.

APPENDIXES

A. METRICAL PATTERNS

Persian versifiers are not rigid adherents to the rules of prosody, which were originally formulated to suit Arabic poetry with its strict differentiation between long and short syllables and its heavy accentuation. In Persian poetry wide variations in the number and succession of syllables are to be found in each foot of a given meter.

For a definition of "length" in syllables see Note 1, page 65. Here, with their metric patterns, are transliterations of some of the originals quoted in translation in the text.

Ruba'i. Quatrain on page 39, "Into this Universe . . .":

— — ᴗ ᴗ — / ᴗ — ᴗ — / — — —
— — ᴗ ᴗ — / ᴗ — ᴗ — / — ᴗ ᴗ —
— — ᴗ ᴗ — / — ᴗ ᴗ — / — ᴗ ᴗ —
— — ᴗ ᴗ — / — ᴗ ᴗ — / — ᴗ ᴗ —

Az amadanam/nabud ᴗ gard/unra sud
waz raftanam/jalal u jah/ash nafzud
Waz hich kasi/niz ᴗ dugush/am nashnud
kin amadan u/raftanam az/bahri chi bud.

Ghazal. Ghazal on page 113, "Where is the glad news . . .":

— ᴗ ᴗ̱ — / ᴗ ᴗ — — / ᴗ ᴗ — — / — —
(Repeated throughout.)

Muzhda-i wasl/-i tu ku kaz/sar-i jan bar/khizam
ta'ir-i quds/am u az dam/-i jahan bar/khizam

175

Bawala-i/tu ki gar ban/-da-i khisham/khani
  az sar-i kha/-jagi-i kawn /u makan bar/khizam
Ya rabb az ab/-ri hidayat/barasan ba/-rani
  pishtar az an/ki chu gardi/zi miyan bar/khizam
Barsar-i tur/-bati man ba/may u mutrib/banshin
  ta ba-buyat/zi lahad raqs/◡ kunan bar/khizam
Khiz u bala/ba-numa ay/but-i shirin/harakat
  kaz sar-i jan/u jahan dast/◡ fishan bar/khizam
Garchi pir-am/tu shabi tang/◡ dar aghush/-am kash
  ta sahargah/zi kanar-i/tu jawan bar/khizam
Ruz-i margam/nafasi muh/lat-i didar/◡ ba-dih
  ta chu Hafiz/zi dar-i jan/u jahan bar/khizam.

Qasida. The arrangement of lines and rhymes in the qasida is the same as for the ghazal, but it is generally longer and its meters may be different.

Mathnavi. This form is used for romantic, epic, didactic, and other poems whose theme demands considerable length and so makes the use of a single rhyme throughout difficult, if not impossible. Each line is made up of two halves which rhyme together. The first specimen given here is from the *Shahnama* (translated on page 73, "There he saw a maiden . . ."):

  ◡ — — / ◡ — — / ◡ — — / ◡ — —

Yaki dukh/-tari did/◡ bar san/-i mah
Furu hish/-ta az charkh/◡ dalwi/ba chah
Chu an mah/◡ rukh ru/-yi Shahpur/◡ did
bayamad/ baru af/-rin gus/-tarid
Ki shadan/badi shad/u khandan/badi
hama sa/-la az bi/gazandan/ badi
Kunun bi/guman tish/-na bashad/sutur
badin dih/buwad ab/◡ yak ru/-y shur.

  The *Mathnavi-i Ma'navi* of Jalal al-Din Rumi (translated on page 108, "List to the reed . . .") provides a further example:

  — ◡ — — / — ◡ — — / — ◡ —

Bashnaw az may/chun hikayat/mikunad
az juda'i/-ha shikayat/mikunad
Kaz nayistan/ta mara bab/-rida and
az nafiram/mard u zan na/-lida and

176

S'ina khaham/sharha sharha/az firaq
ta baguyam/sharh-i dard-i/ishtiyaq
Har kasi ku/dur ⌣ mand az/asl-i khish
baz ⌣ juyad/ruz ⌣ gar-i/wasl-i khish.

B. PERSIAN WRITERS

The following is a list of Persian writers, containing general
biographical information supplementary to that contained in
the text.

Abū Sa'īd ibn Abū'l-Khair. "Pivot of Sufism" at Nīshāpūr.
Died A.D. 1049. Author of early rubā'īyāt of mystical content.

Anṣārī of Herāt. Known as "Pīr-i Herāt"; one of the best and
oldest composers of Ṣūfī quatrains. He died A.D. 1088.

Anvarī, Auḥad al-Dīn. Qaṣīda writer, eulogist, and satirist.
Served the Seljuq sultan of Khurasan (A.D. 1117–1157) and
died about 1190.

Asadī of Ṭūs. A *dihqan* and apologist of the Iranian aristocracy
against the Arabs. Author of *Lughat-i Furs*, the oldest known
dictionary of Persian, and of an epic, *Garshāsp-nāma*, composed
A.D. 1064–1066 and dedicated to a trans-Caucasian prince of
Nakhchawān.

'Aṭṭār, Farīd al-Dīn. Born at Nīshāpūr; died A.D. 1220,
though other dates are given. Author of numerous Ṣūfī
mathnavīs, of which the best known is the *Manṭiq al-Ṭair*
(*The Language of the Birds*). The variety of the works ascribed
to him is so great that doubt has been cast upon his authorship
of some.

Bal'amī, Abū 'Alī Muḥammad. Minister to the Sāmānid shah,
Manṣūr ibn Nūh (reigned A.D. 961–976), for whom he trans-
lated Tabarī's history from Arabic into Persian. He died in
A.H. 386 (= A.D. 996).

Daulatshāh of Samarqand. Wrote a standard biographical
dictionary of poets (*Tadhkirat al-Shu'arā*) in 1487, when he
was about fifty years old. His facts are not always reliable,
but his style is straightforward and his matter interesting.

Firdausī, Abū'l-Qāsim Ḥasan(or Manṣūr). Born near Ṭūs (in
Khurasan), of which he was a *dihqan*. He spent twenty-five
years on the composition of the *Shāhnāma*, the great epic

which deals with the annals of Persia from mythical times down to the Muhammadan invasion of Iran and the overthrow of the Sasanian dynasty. He died A.D. 1020, or possibly five years later.

Gurgānī (Fakhrī of Gurgān). Author of *Wīs u Rāmīn*, a romantic poem on the loves of Wīs and Rāmīn composed between A.D. 1040 and 1054. It was an Oriental counterpart of the Tristan and Isolde romance. Wīs is the wife of King Maubad of Merv, and Rāmīn, his brother.

Ḥāfiẓ of Shīrāz. The best known of the ghazal writers, and the last of the true Ṣūfī poets. Died A.D. 1389 or 1390. See under "Ḥāfiẓ" in list of works in translation.

Hujwīrī, 'Alī b. 'Uthmān. Born at Ghazni (Afghanistan) about the beginning of the eleventh century and died about 1070. Author of *Kashf al-Maḥjūb* (*q.v.*) and other works.

'Irāqī (Fakhr al-Dīn of Hamadān). A mystic whose most characteristic work, *Lama'āt* (*Flashes*), reveals in a mixture of prose and verse the ecstasies to which the Ṣūfī can be subject. Died A.D. 1289.

Jāmī, Nur al-Dīn 'Abd al-Raḥmān. Born at Jām, a township in the district of Herāt, once capital of the province of Khurasan, in 1414. Author of numerous works of religious (often Ṣūfī) content, three dīvāns of lyrical verse, the septet of mathnavīs called *Haft Aurang* (*The Seven Thrones*) and the *Bahāristān* (*Abode of Spring*), a book of didactic essays in a mixture of prose and verse imitating Sa'dī's *Gulistān*. Most of his work is derivative or based on older models. He died A.D. 1492.

Juvainī, 'Alā al-Dīn 'Aṭā. Born at Juvain (western Khurasan) A.D. 1225 and entered the service of the Mongol government as a youth. Accompanied Hulagu on his campaign against the Assassins and in 1259 was made governor of Baghdad. Compiled *Ta'rīkh-i-Jahān Gushā* (a history of the Mongols from the rise of Chingiz Khan down to A.D. 1256) and died in 1283.

Khāqānī of Shīrwān (Caucasus). Born about A.D. 1126. Rivaled Anwarī for his skill in the composition of panegyric qaṣīdas. Made the pilgrimage to Mecca, one of the literary results being *Tuḥfat al-'Irāqain* (*Gift of the Two 'Irāqs*), the first Persian book of travel composed in mathnavī form. He died, after an adventurous life, in 1199.

Mustaufī, Hamd Allāh, Qazvīnī. State accountant in the service of the Īl Khān dynasty of Persia. Compiled *Tārīkh-i Guzīda*, a general history from the Creation down to A.H. 730 (= A.D. 1329–1330), *Nuzhat al-Qulūb*, a cosmography of Persia and adjacent countries, and other works.

Nāṣir-i Khusrau of Merv. Traveler, skeptic, and poet. Born A.D. 1004 at Merv (Khurasan); other particulars of his career uncertain. It is probable that on a pilgrimage to Mecca he was converted to the heretic Ismā 'īlī (Shī'a) sect and entered the service of the Fāṭimid caliph of Egypt, Mustanṣir (A.D. 1035–1094). As a trained missioner for the sect he returned to his native province, where he came into conflict with officers of the Seljuq sultans, who were Sunnī (orthodox) in their beliefs. He took refuge in an obscure village in Badakhshan and there died, probably in 1077. Many legends gathered about him, and it is not always certain that he was responsible for all the literary works which bear his name. Amongst others ascribed to him are the *Traveler's Provision*, a long prose work of theology and philosophy combined; a dīvān; and a travel diary (*Safar-nama, q.v.*).

Niẓāmī 'Arūḍi of Samarqand. Flourished in the first half of the twelfth century. A poet and courtier who spent his life in the capital cities of Khurasan and Transoxiana. Author of *Chahār Maqāla (q.v.)*.

'Omar Khayyām. Mathematician and astrologer-astronomer. Famed in the West for his mystico-philosophical quatrains, translated and combined by Edward FitzGerald into the *Rubā'īyāt*. Said to have died A.D. 1123.

Rūdakī, Ja'far ibn Muhammad. "The first to produce good poetry in Persian." Born at Rūdak, near Samarqand, he served the Sāmānids as court poet and died in A.H. 329 (= A.D. 940–941).

Rūmī, Maulavi Jalāl al-Dīn. Born at Balkh (Khurasan), A.D. 1207. The most prolific Ṣūfī poet in Persian literature. Settled in Konia (Rūm). Author of *Mathnavī-i Ma'navī, Divāni Shams-i Tabrīz*, and others. Died A.D. 1273.

Sa'dī of Shīrāz, commonly called "Sheik." Born about A.D. 1189. After an adventurous life, he settled in his native

Shīrāz. Author of *Būstān, Gulistān,* and numerous ghazals and qaṣīdas. Died about A.D. 1291, at any rate at a phenomenally advanced age.

Sanā'ī of Ghazna. A mystical poet, forerunner of Farīd al-Dīn 'Aṭṭār. He lived at the court of the Ghaznavid sultan Bahrām Shāh and died before the middle of the twelfth century. Author of *Ḥadīqat al-Ḥaqīqa* (*The Garden of Truth*) and other mathnavīs, as well as of a dīvān.

PERSIAN WORKS IN
TRANSLATION

Persian texts established on modern standards of scholarship are the product of the past hundred years. Printing—in the form of lithography—was not introduced into Persia until about 1816, so that translations made until then, and for long afterward, were from texts in manuscript form, often uncertain.

The following is a list of titles published in the last hundred years, with a few earlier works of interest added. It should be noted that the transliteration of Persian/Arabic names and works varies according to the language and personal taste of the translator.

Anwāri Suhailī. A Persian paraphrase of the anonymous Fables of Bidpai (*Kalīla wa-Dimna*), literally translated into prose and verse, by E. B. Eastwick. Hertford, 1854.

The Anwar-i-Suhaili, or *Lights of Canopus*. An anonymous work translated from the Persian by A. N. Wollaston. London, 1877.

Arifī of Herāt. *The Ball and the Polo-stick*, or *The Book of Ecstasy* (*Gūy u Chaugān*). Translated by R. S. Greenshields. London, 1932. A tragic poem describing the passionate affection entertained by a dervish for a prince.

Asadī (Junior) of Ṭūs. *Le Livre de Gerchasp*. Translated and published by Cl. Huart. First edition, Paris, 1926.

'Aṭṭār, Farīd al-Dīn. *The Conference of the Birds* (*Manṭiq al-Ṭair*). An abridged version of the Ṣūfī allegory by R. P. Masani. London, 1924.

—— *Le Livre des conseils* (*Pand-nameh*). Translated into French and published by Silvestre de Sacy. Paris, 1819.

'Aṭṭār, Farīd al-Dīn. *Tadhkirat al-Auliyá* (memorial of the saints). English translation by A. J. Arberry entitled *Muslim Saints and Mystics*. Chicago and London, 1966. A biographical dictionary of Ṣūfīs.

Avicenna. *Le Livre de Science (Dānish-nāma)*. Vol. I: *Logique, Métaphysique*. Vol. II: *Physique, Mathématiques*. French translation by Moh. Achena and Henri Massé. Paris, 1955, 1958.

Firdausī, Abū'l Qāsim Ḥasan. *The Epic of Kings*. Stories retold from Firdausī by Helen Zimmern. London, 1882.

—— *The Shah Nameh of the Persian poet Firdausi*. Translated and abridged in prose and verse, with notes and illustrations, by J. Atkinson. London, 1832.

—— *The Shahnama of Firdausi*. English verse translation by A. G. Warner . . . and E. Warner. 9 vols. London, 1905–1925.

—— *The Shah-namah of Fardusi*. Translated by A. Rogers. London, 1907.

—— *The Shah-nama or "Epic of the Kings."* Translated by Reuben Levy. Chicago and London, 1966.

Gurgānī (Fakhrī of Gurgān). *Le Roman de Wîs et Râmîn (Wîs u Râmîn)*. Translated by Henri Massé. Paris, 1959.

Ḥāfiẓ of Shīrāz. *The Divan*. Translated for the first time from the Persian into English prose by H. Wilberforce Clarke. 3 vols. Calcutta, 1891.

—— *Fifty Poems of Ḥāfiẓ*. Texts and translations by A. J. Arberry. Cambridge, 1947.

—— *Poems from the Divan of Hafiz*. Translated by Gertrude L. Bell. London, 1897.

—— *The Poems of Shemseddin Mohammed Hafiz of Shiraz*. J. Payne, London, 1901.

Hedayat (Sadeq). *The Blind Owl (Būf-e Kūr)*. Written in 1930; translated by D. P. Costello. New York and London, 1961. ("A succession of opium dreams, mystical experiences, and sexual fancies. Simple, often elegant, style.")

Hujwīrī, 'Alī b. 'Uthmān. *Kashf-al-Mahjub*. Translated by Reynold A. Nicholson, E. J. W. Gibb Memorial Series, London, 1911. A discussion of the doctrines of the Ṣūfīs, with a Persian flavor of philosophical speculation.

'Irāqī (Fakhr al-Dīn of Hamadān). *The Songs of Lovers* ('*Ushshāq-Nāma*). Edited and translated into verse by A. J. Arberry. Oxford, 1939.

Jāmī, Nur al-Dīn 'Abd al-Raḥmān. *Bahāristān* (*Persian Wit and Humour*). The sixth book of the *Bahāristān* of Jāmī, translated for the first time from the original Persian by C. E. Wilson. London, 1883.

—— *The Book of Joseph and Zuleikha by Mullana Abdulrahman Jami.* Historical romantic Persian poem translated into English verse by A. Rogers. London, 1892, 1910.

—— *FitzGerald's Salaman and Absal.* Edited by A. J. Arberry. London, 1956. FitzGerald's two translations (1856 and 1879) of *Salaman and Absal* into English verse with a literal translation of the poem and an introduction by Professor Arberry.

—— *Lawā'iḥ.* A facsimile of an old manuscript of a treatise on Sufism by Jāmī, with a translation by E. H. Whinfield. London, 1891.

—— *Salaman and Absal.* An allegory translated from the Persian by Edward FitzGerald. Boston, 1899; London, 1904.

—— *Salaman wa Absal.* An allegory translated from the Persian by F. Falconer. London, 1856.

—— *Yusuf and Zulaikha.* A poem translated into English verse by R. T. H. Griffith. London, 1882.

Juvaini, 'Alā al-Dīn 'Aṭā. *History of the World-Conqueror* (*Ta'rīkh-i-Jahān Gushā*). Translated by J. A. Boyle. 2 vols. Manchester, England, and Cambridge, Mass., 1958.

Kai Kā'ūs ibn Iskandar ibn Qābūs. *Qābūs-nāma* (or *Andarz-nāma*). Translated from the Persian under the title *A Mirror for Princes* by Reuben Levy. London, 1951. A book of practical counsel from a father (Kai Kā'ūs ibn Iskandar ibn Qābūs) to his son. The original was completed A.D. 1082.

Kāshifī, Husain Wā'iz. *The Morals of the Beneficent* (*Akhlāq-i Muṣhinī*). A manual of ethics, literally translated by H. G. Keene. Hertford, 1850.

Mustaufī, Hamd Allāh, Qazvīnī. *Nuzhat al-Qulūb.* A cosmography dealing principally with Persia and adjacent countries. The geographical part is translated by G. le Strange, E. J. W. Gibb Memorial Series. London, 1919.

—— *Tārīkh-i Guzīda.* A general history from the Creation to A.H. 730 (= A.D. 1329–1330), abridged in English, by

183

Edward G. Browne, E. J. W. Gibb Memorial Series. London, 1913.

Nāṣir-i Khusrau. *Sefer-Nameh (Safar-nama)*. Relation du voyage, publié, traduit, et annoté par Ch. Schefer. Paris, 1881.

Niẓām al-Mulk. *The Book of Government or Rules for Kings (Siyāsat-nāma)*. Translated from the Persian by Hubert Darke. London, 1960; New Haven, Conn., 1961.

Niẓāmi 'Arūḍi of Samarqand. *Chahār Maqāla (Four Discourses)*. A translation by Edward G. Browne of the four discourses on secretaries, poets, astrologers, and physicians. E. J. W. Gibb Memorial Series. London, 1921.

Niẓāmī of Ganja. *Ferhad und Schirin (Khusrau u Shīrīn)*. Die literarische Geschichte eines persischen Sagenstoffes, text und Übersetzung von H. W. Duda. Prague, 1933.

—— *Lailī and Majnūn*. A poem from the original Persian by J. Atkinson. London, 1836.

—— *The Seven Beauties (Haft Paikar)*. Translated by C. E. Wilson. Parts I and II. London, 1924.

—— *The Sikandar Nama (Book of Alexander the Great)*. Translated into prose by H. Wilberforce Clarke. London, 1881.

—— *The Treasury of Mysteries*. Translated by G. H. Darab. London, 1945.

'Omar Khayyām. *Edward FitzGerald's Ruba'iyat of Omar Khayyam*. A close prose and verse translation with a Persian text by Eben Francis Thompson. Worcester, Mass., 1907.

—— *The Quatrains of Omar Khayyam*. The Persian text with an English verse translation by E. H. Whinfield. London, 1883; second edition, 1901.

—— *Rubā'īyāt*. Edited from a newly discovered manuscript dated A.H. 658 (= A.D. 1259–1260) by A. J. Arberry, with comparative English versions by Edward FitzGerald, E. H. Whinfield, and the Editor. London, 1949. There is also a new version, based upon recent discoveries, by A. J. Arberry. London, 1951.

—— *Ruba'iyat*. English, French, and German translations comparatively arranged in accordance with the text of Edward FitzGerald's version, collected and edited by N. H. Dole. Boston, 1896.

Rashīd al-Dīn Faḍl Allāh. *Histoire Universelle (Jāmiʿal-Tavārīkh)*. Persian text, with French translation and annotation by K. Jahn. Leiden, 1951. An English translation by J. A. Boyle is in preparation.

The Regions of the World (Ḥudud al-ʿĀlam). Translated and annotated by V. Minorsky. E. J. W. Gibb Memorial Series. London, 1937. An anonymous geographical work compiled A.D. 982–983 and dedicated to a prince living in what is now northern Afghanistan.

Rūmī, Maulavī Jalāl al-Dīn. *The Masnavi: Book II*. Translated from the Persian into prose by C. E. Wilson. London, 1910.

—— *Mathnavī-i Maʿnavī*. Translation and commentary by Reynold A. Nicholson, E. J. W. Gibb Memorial Series. London, 1926–1940.

—— *The Mesnevi: Book the First*. Translated and the poetry versified by J. W. Redhouse. London, 1881.

—— *More Tales from the Masnavi*. Selected and translated by A. J. Arberry. London, 1963.

—— *The Rubāʿiyāt*. Selected translations into English verse by A. J. Arberry. London, 1949.

—— *Selected Poems from the Divani Shamsi Tabriz*. Edited and translated by Reynold A. Nicholson. Cambridge, 1898. A new translation by A. J. Arberry is in preparation.

—— *The Spiritual Couplets (Masnavi i Maʿnavi)*. Translated and abridged by E. H. Whinfield. London, 1898.

—— *The Table-talk of Jalāl al-Dīn Rūmī (Fīhi mā fīhi)*. Selections translated from the Persian by R. A. Nicholson. Ed. A. J. Arberry. London, 1951.

Saʿdī of Shīrāz. *The Bustan*. Translated for the first time into prose, with explanatory notes and index, by H. Wilberforce Clarke. London, 1879.

—— *The Bustan*. Translated into English by Ziauddin Gulam Moheiddin Munshi, revised by Rochfort Davies. Bombay, 1889.

—— *The Bustan of Sadi*. Translated from the Persian with an introduction by A. Hart Edwards. London, 1911.

—— *Flower-garden (Gulistan)*. Translated by James Ross. London, 1823.

Sa'dī of Shīrāz. *The Gulistan.* Translated in prose and verse by Sir E. Arnold. London, 1899.

—— *Rose Garden (The Gulistan).* Translated into prose and verse by E. B. Eastwick. Hertford, 1852.

—— *Rose Garden (The Gulistan).* Translated by Francis Gladwin. Calcutta, 1845.

—— *Rose Garden (The Gulistan).* Translated from a revised text by J. T. Platts. London, 1873.

—— *Stories from the Bustan of Shaykh Sa'di.* With selections from Francis Gladwin's translation of Sa'dī's *Gulistān*, the former translated and the latter revised by Reuben Levy. London, 1928.

Ṣanā'ī of Ghazna. *The first Book of the Hadiqatu'l Haqiqat or The Enclosed Garden of the Truth (Ḥadīqat al-Ḥaqīqa).* Edited and translated by Major J. Stephenson. Calcutta, 1910.

Shabistarī, (Maḥmūd). *Gulshan-i Raz (The Mystic Rose Garden).* The Persian text, with an English translation by E. H. Whinfield. London, 1880.

Tadhkirat al-Mulūk. Translated and annotated by V. Minorsky. E. J. W. Gibb Memorial Series. London, 1943. An anonymous manual describing the system of governmental administration under the Safavi shahs, dated about 1725.

Ṭāhir, Bābā. *The Lament of Baba Tahir.* Edited and translated by E. Heron-Allen, and rendered into English verse by Elizabeth Curtis Brenton. London, 1902.

—— *Poems of a Persian Sufi.* The quatrains of Bābā Ṭāhir, translated by A. J. Arberry. Cambridge, 1937.

Ṭūsi, Nāṣir al-Dīn. *Nasirean Ethics (Akhlaq-i Nasiri).* Translated by G. W. Wickens. London, 1964.

'Ubaid Zākānī. *Rats against Cats (Mūsh u Gurba).* Translated by Mas'ūd Farzād. London, 1946.

Varavini. *Tales of Marzuban (Marzubannama).* Translated by Reuben Levy. London and Bloomington, Indiana, 1959.

INDEX

Abaqa, 59
Abbasids, 9, 19–23
Abd Allah Dhu'l-Yaminain, 23, 47
Abode of Spring, The (Jami), 159–60
Abu Bakr, 17
Abu Ishaq Inju, 128, 150
Abu'l-Abbas, 19
Abu'l-'Abbas Isfara'ini, 80
Abu Mansur, son of Abd al-Razzaq, 49
Abu Mansur al-Mu'ammari, quoted, 49–50
Abu Sa'id, Sultan, 152
Abu Sa'id ibn Abu'l-Khair, 36–38, 41
Abu Shukur of Balkh, 36
Abu Tammam, 47
Achaemenian dynasty, 4–7
Aesop's Fables, 109
Afrasiyab, 74–75
Afshin, 48
Ahriman, 11, 16
Ahura Mazda, 6, 11, 16
Ala al-Din Muhammad, 32
Alexander the Great, 89
Allah, 16, 40
Ali (first imam of the Shiites), 18

'Ali Shir Nawa'i, 159
Allegory, 98–99, 129–30
Amir Khusrau of Delhi, 173
Amr ibn Laith, 25
Andarz-nama (Book of Counsel) (Kai Ka'us), 52–53
Anecdotes, 108–9
"Annals of the Apostles and Kings" (Tabari), 47–48
Anonymity, 40
'Anqa, 104, 104n
Anvari, 32, 127, 148–49
Arabian Nights, 63
Arabic, 15–16, 21, 22, 48–49
Arabs, invasion by, 12–19
Aramaic, 5–6
Architecture, 161
Arif Zazvini, 164–65
Arnold, Matthew, 68
Asadi of Tus, 42
Atabegs, 60
'Attar, Farid al-Din, 97–102
Avesta, 6–7
Avicenna, 104, 104n

Bahar, 163–65
Baharistan (The Abode of Spring) (Jami), 159–60
Bahram Chubin, 25

187

Mazdak, 11
Mazdak, Book of, 48
Metaphor, 83
Meter, 65, 65n, 175–76
Miniature-painting, 161
Minstrelsy, Kai Ka'us on, 52–53
Minuchihr, 67
Mirza, Iraj, 164–65
Monorhyme, 42
Muhammad, Prophet, 17, 59
Muhammad Shah, 162
Muhtasib (censor), 132
Mujahid al-Din, 132
Mulla Jami, 64
Musa (Moses), 111, 125
Musibat-nama (The Book of Travail) (Farid al-Din 'Attar), 98, 101–2
Mustansir, Caliph, 139
Mutaqarib, 65, 65n
Mysticism: in Jalal al-Din Rumi, 105; in Sa'di of Shiraz, 124; in Hafiz of Shiraz, 129, 131; in Jami, 159

Nafahat al-Uns (Zephyrs of Tranquillity) (Jami), 159
Nasir al-Din, King, 162
Nasir Khusrau of Merv: life of, 135–39; Ismailism of, 137; quoted, 137–39; skepticism of, 140–41; pseudo-autobiography of, 141–45; travel narrations of, 145–46
Nawa'i, 'Ali Shir, 159
Nihawand, battle of, 12–13
Nizam al-Mulk, 53–54, 61
Nizami, Jalal al-Din Ilyas ibn Yusuf: and use of

Nizami, *(Continued)*
legend, 80–81; and craftsmanship, 81; synopsis of works of, 82–92
Nizami of Ganja, 64
Novel, 169

Odes, 103–4
Omar, Caliph, 17
Omar Khayyam, 36, 38–42
One-ness, 104

Panj Ganj (Five Treasures) (Nizami), 81–92, 159
Pakistan, Persian language in, 172
Panegyrics, 25–26, 29, 31–32, 128, 163
Pantheism, 36
Parthians, 5
Pazand, 120n
Pehlevi (Middle Persian), 2, 5–6, 15, 21, 47
Persia: geography and commerce, 3–4
Persian, Islamic, 2, 22
Philosophy, practical, 7
Poetry: vs. prose, 34; didactic, 43, 97, 163–64; moral, 61; pastoral, 71; erotic, 81; religous, 162
Poets, court, 26, 28–29, 98, 149
"Politician, The" (Jamalzadeh), quoted, 169–71
Prose, secular, 48–49

Qa'ani, 162–63
Qabus-nama (Book of Qabus) (Kai Ka'us), 32, 34, 52–53
Qadir, Caliph, 142
Qara Khita'i, 60
Qazvin, 109–10